Managing Women

OPEN UNIVERSITY PRESS
Gender and Education Series

Editors
ROSEMARY DEEM
Professor of Educational Research, University of Lancaster
GABY WEINER
Professor of Education, Umea University, Sweden

The series provides compact and clear accounts of relevant research and practice in the field of gender and education. It is aimed at trainee and practising teachers, and parents and others with an educational interest in ending gender inequality. All age-ranges will be included, and there will be an emphasis on ethnicity as well as gender. Series authors are all established educational practitioners or researchers.

TITLES IN THE SERIES

Managing Women
Sue Adler, Jenny Laney and Mary Packer

Boys Don't Cry
Sue Askew and Carol Ross

Science and Technology in the Early Years
Naima Browne (ed.)

Untying the Apron Strings
Naima Browne and Pauline France (eds)

Changing Perspectives on Gender
Helen Burchell and Val Millman (eds)

Co-education Reconsidered
Rosemary Deem (ed.)

Women Teachers
Hilary de Lyon and Frances Widdowson Migniuolo (eds)

Girls and Sexuality
Lesley Holly (ed.)

Women in Educational Management
Jenny Ozga

A History of Women's Education in England
June Purvis

Shaping Up to Womanhood
Sheila Scraton

Whatever Happens to Little Women?
Christine Skelton (ed.)

Dolls and Dungarees
Eva Tutchell (ed.)

Just a Bunch of Girls
Gaby Weiner (ed.)

Women and Training
Ann Wickham

Managing Women

FEMINISM AND POWER IN EDUCATIONAL MANAGEMENT

Sue Adler, Jenny Laney and Mary Packer

Open University Press
Buckingham • *Philadelphia*

Open University Press
Celtic Court
22 Ballmoor
Buckingham
MK18 1XW

email: enquiries@openup.co.uk
world wide web: http://www.openup.co.uk

and

325 Chestnut Street
Philadelphia, PA 19106, USA

First Published 1993
Reprinted 1995, 1999

A catalogue record of this book is available from the British Library.

ISBN 0 335 15780 7

Library of Congress Cataloging-in-Publication Data

Adler, Sue, 1948–
      Managing women: feminism and power in educational
   management/Sue Adler, Jenny Laney, Mary Packer.
         p.   cm. — (Gender and education)
      Includes bibliographical references and index.
      ISBN 0–335–15780–7
      1. Women school administrators — Great Britain.   2. Women in
   education — Great Britain.   I. Laney, Jenny, 1947–   . II. Packer,
   Mary, 1949–   .   III. Title.   IV. Series: Gender and education series.
   LB2831.826.G7A36   1993
   371.2'01'082 — dc20   92–34666
                                                                       CIP

Typeset by Colset Pte Ltd, Singapore
Printed in Great Britain by J.W. Arrowsmith Ltd, Bristol

To Stephanie Louise

Contents

Series Editor's Introduction

I am particularly pleased to be able to introduce this book as I was in at its inception. I was tutor to the authors when they were researching and writing their joint MA dissertation and quickly recognized the exhilaration and also the meticulous planning and continuous commitment that this kind of work demanded. The pros and cons of embarking on a joint MA dissertation have yet to be written up, but the commitment to feminist ways of working which went into the decision to embark on such a joint venture is also very evident in this, the publication of a much revised and expanded version of that work.

Issues relating to management and women have become increasingly high profile across the political spectrum: so much so that recently, even the British Conservative Prime Minister, John Major, gave his support for more senior women in management in a well-publicized government-initiated project *Opportunity 2000*. However, while there are some excellent volumes on women and management, for example, the collection edited by Jenny Ozga (1992) in this series, few have been written from an explicitly feminist standpoint.

Thus, this volume is unusual compared with others on women and management for a number of reasons. First, it moves away from the view that women-as-managers are somehow a 'good thing' and towards wishing to understand how the complex relationships of power within educational institutions affect women who may also be managers. Second, the authors make the distinction between 'women in management' (who may have little sympathy with feminism) and 'feminists in management', a point often ignored by other publications on the subject.

And third, they devote a considerable amount of the book to reflecting on their research approach – explicitly feminist in aim, rationale and methodology – and the difficulties and satisfaction which this brought to them.

In my view, then, this volume will interest a wide range of readers: but in particular, two distinct groups – those interested in general issues relating to women and management and those interested in feminist research methods. The first group will find this volume refreshingly different: it is boldly and clearly written, it reports on a carefully planned and executed research study and it challenges as well as confirms some established themes of the literature. For example, it claims that there is a particular female experience of management which differs from that of male managers, that women's attitude to power is ambivalent and that promotion, say for teachers out of the classroom, may be viewed with suspicion because it implies having to take on 'male' ways of working.

Those interested in feminist research methods will be able to compare the considered reflections on the workings of a feminist project, in this book, with those of others such as Stanley and Wise (1983). Feminists have long challenged the objectivist 'scientific' approach of much social science research and here the authors share similar views to other feminist researchers. They regard feminist research as political, concerned not only with exploration but also with change; they see themselves as activists, not 'outside' the research but part of it; and they see the complex relationships involved in women researching women.

At a time when feminism and feminist practice is being reconstituted in the free-market, hierarchical individualism of the 1990s, this volume indicates that other legitimate perspectives continue to exist. Also, by offering a critique of the managerialism increasingly being imposed on educational institutions and by suggesting other ways of working, this volume also indicates that the 'fight back' has already begun.

Gaby Weiner

Acknowledgements

Our thanks to:

Anne Corbett, who worked with us on the original research and dissertation.

The women who took part in the study and gave so generously of themselves. Without them, there would not have been a product.

Friends, colleagues, families and partners, who put up with us even when the going was rough.

Sisters and feminists, known and read, who have helped to make us who we are today.

Our thanks, too, to the following people for their permission to reproduce their work:

Rona Chadwick/Cath Tate Cards (Figure 1.1, p. 17), Brian Bagnall (Figure 2.1, p. 24), Angela Martin/Cath Tate Cards (Figure 2.2, p. 27), Ros Asquith (Figure 3.1, p. 51), Marian Lydbrooke (Figure 4.1, p. 70).

Introduction

This book developed from a dissertation written in 1990 for the Open University MA in Education. It was an unusual dissertation, being a joint project researched and written collectively by four women. The subject of the dissertation and its 'daughter' – this book – is women and educational management, in particular, the areas of conflict between feminism and the male-defined power structures of educational organizations. We knew from our own experience of some of the contradictions and compromises for women in senior posts in education and we have looked at some of the ways in which women positively influence management styles in institutions.

We chose the topic of our research for a combination of personal and professional reasons. We all had experience of being managed and of being in managerial positions. We are all feminists. We were – and are – interested in the possibilities of retaining feminist ideologies and idealism while working within a system fundamentally hostile to feminist challenge and change. Compromise on many levels seemed to us inevitable. Feminists working in educational establishments, whatever their degree of radicalism, have to work within the mainstream and often have to modify their feminisms to liberalism and reformism. They aim for what is possible whilst maintaining a vision of the ideal.

In the past few years, senior management positions became a reality for some women, albeit just a few. The recognition that, both as individuals and collectively, women and their approaches can alter the organization, is real. We wanted to find out more about how women with some power fitted into

educational organizations, and how the organizations themselves changed. We were, too, conscious of the important
distinction between 'women in management' and 'feminists in
management'.

Our research project focused entirely on women, and provided us and the women in the study with opportunities to
explore and expose aspects of our feminisms in relation to our
work in education and to management. Searching literature
combining education, management and feminism, we had found
little on the subject and were excited at the thought of venturing
into an area relatively unexplored. Two chapters in the book are
specifically on management; another considers feminism.

Power (often construed as patriarchal power) as negative and
undesirable, is a concept that we as feminists wanted to both
demystify and reconstruct. Current feminist writing appears to
share our wish to re-image power, to look at woman-power.
This is evidenced in titles such as *Power–Gender–Values*,
Women Teaching for Change: Gender, Class and Power and
many, many more. One of our chapters is on power, again
within the context of feminism and educational management.

Our project collected information from eighty-five women
who were working or had worked in education. The majority
had been or were teachers; a minority were librarians, coun-
sellors and media resources officers. Their experiences were in all
phases, from under-fives to higher and adult education. We conducted forty-four face-to-face interviews and received thirty
postal questionnaires and eleven letters. We asked each woman
about her education and career pattern, life-style and family,
feminism, power, management and future plans. Responses
from five women are given in some detail – contributions from
all the women are referred to throughout the book. Quantitative
data is included in the Appendices. The questionnaire and profile
sheet we used is appended, too.

We selected women to interview and placed advertisements
in carefully chosen publications. Our response rate to the
questionnaire was extremely high – we attribute this to our
deliberate targeting. It became obvious at an early stage that
women responded enthusiastically because issues of management are pertinent to them. Many of the responses showed a
strength of feeling that echoed our own. In addition, many
women expressed interest in our collective work process.

Four women with diverse experiences in education chose to work on the research and dissertation. This book was written by three from that original group. We have documented our collaboration, together with theories of feminist methodology, in a chapter as one example of a feminist practice.

We found it hard to make generalizations about the four of us. We were initially tentative about even recognizing the differences; later we came to regard our varied views as positive, a way of keeping the dialogue going, seeing them as complementary and enriching. We are all white women. We have both common and different experiences of identifying ourselves and of oppression, based on social class, sexuality, religion, age, culture, nationality and ethnicity. Two of us are mothers; two, women without children.

The diversity helped us guard against making sweeping statements about groups of women in the research. Women are not, of course, a homogeneous group. Even in one small specific group – for example women in senior positions in education – we found in our study many significant differences as well as some similarities. The eighty-five women presented us with that number of stories. We were not trying to find a 'representative' sample, from whom we may have been tempted to generalize. Rather, using qualitative research methods, we aimed to give these women in education a voice and make them more visible. And from their individual experiences, we ourselves have recognized many threads and mirrors of our own lives.

We have also seen ways forward for educational institutions – ways that have much to do with the sane, sensible and suitable management priorities held by so many of the women in our study.

CHAPTER 1

Management: A Man's World

Within the last twenty years, management (as a concept and practice) has been introduced into education from the worlds of corporate organization, economic enterprise and large bureaucracies. Educational management has followed commercial management with its emphasis on commodities rather than people – outcomes can always be bigger; profits always more. We see in education, especially as a result of the Education Reform Act (ERA) (1988), management styles and systems attempting to make schools more like commercial businesses. This trend has earlier roots. In 1983 the Department of Education and Science issued a circular recommending management training for heads on a model taken from commerce and industry. The style of management training for heads and the trend towards a business model did not escape criticism. For example, *Education plc?* (Maw, 1984), notes a change in the language used, with 'training' replacing 'education'. It questions the idea that heads have a lot to learn from industrial management. It also questions the simple equation that better heads = better schools = better education for children.

Learning is not a commodity, subject to the same analysis as the products of industry and commerce. The huge differences between the aims of industry and commerce on the one hand, and education on the other, are not always acknowledged. Currently, competitive schooling forces educational institutions to invest finance into marketing and image – not children's learning. Promoting and marketing the school, and managing appraisal and human resources are priorities post-ERA. Books on educational management now contain chapters on these issues; courses appear in the *Times Educational Supplement* regularly on similar topics.

The jargon of educational management reflects the 'big business' culture: parents and their children are 'the client group'; staff management has become 'human resource management'; heads of departments are 'middle managers'; librarians are 'learning resource managers', aims and objectives become 'mission statements' and 'institutional development plans'.

The language of accounting has found its way into schools, where performance indicators and success criteria are used in an attempt to reduce children to manufactured objects. Performance indicators are usually quantitative and much that has real meaning in education is difficult to quantify. Measuring a school's performance in terms of attendance rates, truancy rates, examination results and the production of league tables is one way of quantifying but tells us little about the quality of what is learnt and how it is taught. The links between assessment, ability and action are not straightforward. 'Quality control' is not synonomous with quality education. 'Measuring will tell us how tall a child is – it will not make her or him any taller' said a teacher in our study.

Despite enormous attempts to reduce the on-going process of learning to an examination result and a Standard Attainment Target, teachers rarely 'buy into' this simplistic view. The pseudo-scientific and rationalist approach has its uses in skills training but remains of limited value when applied so rigidly to education and learning. By ignoring contradictions and the highly complex ways in which individuals learn we may be able to produce neat documents on 'process' and 'product'. It does not follow that we also produce a more educated, thinking and capable populace. Arguably, alignment with linear models could be seen as collusion with anti-educational forces.

One of the flaws in the structure of this 'businesslike' version (vision?) of management in education lies with teachers' own decisions to enter a profession that has an often elusive and unmeasurable outcome. People become teachers for a range of reasons, but commercial enterprise is rarely one of them. Many have entered education precisely to avoid commerce and industry, though we suspect that this will now change. In our own study, we had not one instance of a woman entering education to get rich or to run a commercially profitable organization.

Since the Education Reform Act (1988) we have seen the greatest changes in education in England and Wales since the 1944 Education Act. The 1988 Act imposed the National Curriculum, national testing, Local Management of Schools and open enrolment; it allowed for schools to opt out of local authority control and it abolished the Inner London Education Authority (ILEA). These changes have brought with them a very different role for managers. It remains to be seen what effect this will have on the percentage of management positions held by women. Will the new roles of educational management, such as marketing and finance, increase the incidences of educational management being seen as a stereotypically male occupation both by interviewing panels and women themselves?

Looking at the literature

We found that most of the literature on educational management and on theories of management and organization ignored women, either by making the assumption that all managers are male or by assuming a 'gender-free' position. This is also true of many current and influential books on school management. A random example – Bertie Everard and Geoffrey Morris (1990) refer throughout their book *Effective School Management* to managers as 'he' with a few exceptions, where s/he is used. A short paragraph at the end of the Preface states:

> Finally, aware of the strong feelings in the teaching profession about the use of male pronouns to refer to teachers of either sex, we crave the indulgence of female readers where we have stuck to such pronouns in the interests of brevity: we know that you make very successful heads and appreciation of your success is one of the items that should cross the learning bridge from school to industry.
>
> (Everard and Morris, 1990, p. xv)

We did find a number of books and articles (often in academic publications held only by larger libraries) on the issues of women in management. Our bibliography records this. In the relatively small literature there is a spectrum. This ranges from a liberal, 'no-difference' view, to research on differences in male and female management styles, to a feminist view of management which redefines the role of the manager and the structure of the organization.

A few key writers

Jill Blackmore, in *Educational Leadership and a Feminist Critique and Reconstruction* (1989) places the consideration of power within the context of educational management.

Lynette Carpenter is one of the few writers to make clear the distinction between women managers and feminist managers. She explores this in *A Discourse on the Care and Handling of Feminist Administrators* (1989).

Judith Glazer, in *Feminism and Professionalism in Teaching and Educational Administration* (1991), discusses feminist theory, methodology and research application, with the emphasis on the relationship between feminism and professionalism and the role of feminist perspectives in transforming teaching and educational administration.

Phoebe Lambert, in *Women into Educational Management* (1989) describes women's ambivalence about the function of management.

Judi Marshall, in *Women Managers: Travellers in a Male World* (1984) describes her own journey from liberal to radical feminism while engaged in research on women managers.

Helen Regan, in *Not for women only: school administration as a feminist activity* (1990) charts her development into educational management and, simultaneously, feminism.

Charol Shakeshaft, in *Women in Educational Administration* (1987), criticizes the androcentric (male as norm) bias of management theory. She has a women-centred approach to education. Her book is one of the few on the subject of women managers in education.

Throughout this book we refer to the literature, either to give support to or contrast with our own research.

Management styles and theories

Most conventional management theory, including educational management has been conceptualized according to four main categories:

1 what motivates people
2 what managers do
3 how they do it
4 how they should do it

Examples are Mintzberg (1973), Tannenbaum and Schmidt (1973) and Blake and Moulton (1964). Again, the assumption is of the manager as male. Mintzberg's research, adapted by Coulson (1987) for use in an educational context, was based on close observation of five male managers. He found that managers performed three main roles, which he termed interpersonal, informational and decisional. Work such as this should be used with caution because it is concerned with providing the basis of a 'scientific' description of management for use in designing systematic training for managers. The underlying rationale is that analysing what managers do and training other people in these skills will lead quite unproblematically to the production of good managers. Whilst it is useful to analyse management skills, this theory does not take account of diversity – different management styles are needed in different situations. Conventional theory is particularly unhelpful for women because it does not lead to any redefining of the role of manager.

Tannenbaum and Schmidt (1973) studied what managers did and considered management styles on a continuum. They suggested that concern for results and concern for relationships were in conflict and the more managers were concerned with one, the less they were concerned with the other. Almost ten years earlier, Blake and Moulton (1964) recognized that both results and relationships were important. They put concern for people and concern for results on a scale of one to nine on the two axes of a graph. An ideal approach was described as one involving motivation and problem-solving, agreeing goals and expecting achievement, facing up to conflict, delegating clearly and team-building. Interestingly, these views reflect what is often seen as a feminist style of management.

Criticisms

Elisabeth Al-Khalifa (1989) argues that the recent dominant influence in education is management and organization theory, which rests on a rationalist approach to the organization of hierarchies. In her view, the managerial model is essentially a technicist model, which stresses school organizational problems as technical ones amenable to rational problem-solving techniques. This produces a male model of management, with which women are unable to identify. She writes that:

> . . . the resistance among these women to identifying themselves as 'managers' is not a simple consequence of a lack of training . . . but a positive statement about self worth and espoused values.
> (Al-Khalifa, 1989, p. 90)

This is hardly surprising if one looks at the evolution of management theory. Charol Shakeshaft criticizes research and theories of educational management for ignoring the issue of gender. She argues that the research on management has an androcentric bias. It makes the assumption that the experiences of males and females are the same and therefore research on males is appropriate for generalizing the female experience. Female experiences, different from the male's, are ignored or diminished. The white male world view is adopted in research on management, as elsewhere. This bias, according to Shakeshaft, is partly caused by the samples for the research being drawn mainly from the corporate world and the military.

Shakeshaft identifies the work of four theorists to illustrate her criticisms:

1 Getzels and Gubas (1954) on role and role conflict. Their work, which drew on the theories of Talcott Parsons, initially excluded women altogether. Later work including women was disparaging, considering women teachers to have no role conflict as they are 'not likely to do better professionally elsewhere.' (p. 53) Getzels and Gubas' initial research was funded by the Air Force and used samples of military personnel.

2 Leader behaviour descriptions (Halpin and Winer, 1957). This study examined and measured leader performance and behaviour. Those designated as leaders occupied positions of formal authority in corporate, academic or military systems. Shakeshaft notes that their questionnaire ignores the actions of females and possible female conceptualization of leadership behaviour.

3 Fiedler (1967) on leadership effectiveness. This research utilized only business, military and industrial spheres in

developing a theory of leadership effectiveness. When Fiedler found that women perceived their co-workers in positive terms (a factor that he previously identified as one sign of a good leader) he dismissed this as women being naïve, and jumping to quick opinions of people based on stereotypes.

4 Maslow's theory of motivation and self-actualization (1943). This theory is problematic for women as it indicates to women that self-actualization can be achieved by sex-role fulfilment or denial, while men are led towards devaluing the experience of the home. Maslow applies a value scale to the different needs. He ranks self-actualization, affiliation and self-esteem in descending order, thus matching traditional male values. Maslow presents the self-actualized woman as one who has made it in a man's world.

Looking now to contemporary issues in management and our own research we cite Margaret Thatcher as an obvious example of Maslow's self-actualized woman. Our research was carried out in the first half of 1990, while she was still Prime Minister. She was mentioned by a number of the women in our study as an example demonstrating all the worst aspects of a woman adopting an authoritarian male management style. With her handbag (exploited by the media as a symbol) making one statement about her femininity and her 'Iron Lady' image making another, she was everything many women in our study said they did not want to be. We were told:

> If women are too tough they get criticized. No-one wants to be considered to be like Mrs Thatcher. She has done a disservice to women as she doesn't let the natural strengths of women show through. She suffers from a lack of approachability, warmth and softness.
>
> (Secondary Head)

> Maggie Thatcher is a politician, not a man or a woman, some women are managers before they are men or women, some people have more humanity about them.
>
> (Further Education Lecturer)

> Some female managers (e.g. Mrs T.) are arrogant, domineering and a disgrace as people. Many achieve their goals and aims by using other women as nannies and cleaners and assume any woman can do as they have done.
>
> (Counsellor)

Margaret Thatcher's influence has been enormous. The face
of British society, including education, changed dramatically
during her period of office; its legacy continues. Increased
emphasis on individuality and competition is reflected in many
areas. (And inconsistencies abound – an example relevant here
being the issue of childcare and women working outside the
home. One the one hand, Thatcher appeared to want to see
women in the labour market; on the other, she was wholly
unsupportive of childcare.) In both social class and gender
terms, she used the argument of individual strengths to succeed.
She was herself successful as a woman in a man's world – and
she did nothing to improve the position of other women.
Ironically, she gave ample proof to the belief that a woman can
take and use power as well – or as badly – as a man.

Women can do it too . . .

Looking back to the literature, we noted some American
research in the 1970s and 1980s that set out to show that
there was no difference between women or men as managers.
Attempts were made to prove that women are no less effective
than men. Tkach's (1980) study as noted in Marshall (1984)
showed that women are 'no less qualified psychologically for
positions in management than men' (Marshall, 1984, p. 15). This
might be characterized as representing the liberal feminist tradition, trying to show that there is little difference in the way that
women and men manage and indicating that women can achieve
success in the male world by assuming a 'gender-neutral' (i.e.
male) stance and by accepting androcentricity.

Describing herself as 'definitely a feminist, I believe that
women can do virtually everything a man can do' a senior
woman working in Higher Education in our study said:

> I suspect there is no difference . . . Men are better at thinking
> about some aspects of management but . . . the differences
> between men and women are not as great as has been implied.
> They are social constructions rather than natural differences.

She defined the qualities of a good manager as:

- being decisive;
- making up your mind quickly;

- having clear objectives;
- thinking things through in strategic terms rather than getting bogged down in nuts and bolts, which should be delegated to those lower down the system;
- being a good delegator;
- not interfering in other people's work;
- being a good judge of people and what they can do, and addressing those who deviate or buck the system;
- being efficient and well organized, and not continually changing the system, or your mind – sticking to things.

She defined leadership as:

> . . . providing people with a sense of direction, giving them praise and a sense of achievement when they do something well, being willing to tell them and help them improve their performance when they do it badly.

She emphasized that both women and men had these qualities. However, it seems to us and most of the women in our study that men and women chose to use their positions as managers and leaders and therefore their power quite differently.

Judi Marshall cites a study by Schein (1976) that gives evidence of the stereotyping of management as a male occupation and notes, therefore, that women are disadvantaged. Schein's article is 'provocatively' entitled 'Think manager – think male':

> Using a 92 item checklist she [Schein] asked 300 male middle-managers in various U.S. insurance companies and later 167 similar female middle-managers, to describe their perceptions of 'women in general', 'men in general' or 'successful middle managers.' Both samples saw a large and statistically significant resemblance between 'men' and 'managers' . . . The female sample reported a weaker resemblance between 'women' and 'managers' and the male sample a near zero correspondence between the two.
>
> (Marshall, 1984, p. 24)

Schein, according to Marshall, reports that the resemblance of manager to male was most strongly expressed by women with limited management experiences. She suggests that women go through an initial phase in which they try to copy men although this may be replaced with the women developing their own style at a later stage. Schein concludes that women will be discouraged from thinking of management as a career because they do not identify strongly with the role, while those women who are accepted may find it difficult to achieve a viable self-image and style. Catherine Marshall (1985) makes an observation similar to Schein's on gender and management style. She notes that women are more likely to evolve their own management style, as opposed to copying a male style, once they have been in a position for some time. She describes how women go from a management role that is culturally defined, i.e. follows a male model, through a transition to one that is self defined.

Judi Marshall indicates that there are problems with the interpretation of Schein's findings and that they were susceptible to misinterpretations and misuses. We believe that work that underlines the differences between male and female experiences can be used to prove or disprove points across the political spectrum. We are aware of this paradox in interpretations of our own research. Clearly, as feminists, we appreciate the difference in some women's management styles and we make much of the gendered aspects of working with people. As Chapter 7 indicates, some women in our study identified – and preferred – feminine management styles and strategies.

Adam Westoby (1988), describing the micropolitics of schools and institutions, lists strategies used by individuals and groups to exert power and influence over others. We found these an interesting contrast to those noted on the previous page by the senior woman in Higher Education. Westoby's list includes

- establishing norms that deny 'outsiders' competence;
- protective myths;
- secrecy;
- control over selection/recruitment/training;
- distortion of information;
- imposition of rules/regulations/procedures;
- control of rewards;
- losing recommendations by referring them to others in the hope that they will disappear or change beyond all recognition;
- rigging agendas;
- massaging minutes;
- nobbling individuals (using emotive force);
- interpreting the opinions of others.

Westoby considers that these interests could be pursued by groups based on age, sex, race, politics, trade union activities, etc. Each of these groups is an interest group, and could use any or all of the above strategies to gain and keep control. Feminists might dispute this, regarding these as typically masculine ways of relating and working, and easily recognizable to all who work in education. We hope to show that women, and in particular feminists, seek alternatives.

Natasha Josefowitz's book *Paths to Power: A Woman's Guide From First Job To Top Executive* (1980) is one of many aimed at helping women get to management positions and succeed in a man's world. The author focuses on women, although without adopting a feminist perspective. Josefowitz's book, and others such as Cameron (1990) *The Competitive Woman*, and Bryce (1989) *The Influential Woman: How to Achieve Success Without Losing your Femininity*, are available in high street bookshops, as are articles in magazines such as *Cosmopolitan*. Ideas contained in this sort of literature are often used on management training courses aimed at women. Josefowitz writes in her preface, 'This book is about how women can succeed in today's organisations. It is not about how organisations should be or how women should change them.' She does, however, go on to say that she hopes that women will use the power they gain to help other women in lower paid or dead-end jobs. She refers to the work of Blake and Moulton and notes that, in order to overcome stereotypes about women, successful women have sometimes over-compensated for their human concerns by becoming over-concerned with production, instead of trying to achieve a balance.

Many of these publications, aimed at women managers, advise women to act like men, not to cry and to dress for success. Advice is given to women to minimize their femininity in behaviour and in dress. For example:

> To become an executive you must look like what others expect a woman executive to look like. Always be understated, never flashy. Underplay hips and bosom, don't accentuate curves. Wear clothes that allow you to cross your legs comfortably. It's best to err on the side of formality.
>
> (Josefowitz, 1980, p. 78)

Many women in our study responded with enthusiasm and humour to a question on dress codes and power dressing. Some stated that they dressed for comfort, although this did not mean they dressed informally. Several commented on 'dressing-down' and dressing in a 'non-provocative' way, considering this as a way to being taken seriously as managers. (We comment further on image and presentation in Chapter 6.)

Compromising positions

Women often have to make compromises, using male techniques to gain recognition or as a means of self-defence. Forrest (1989) comments on the difficulties that women face because men define what makes a good manager and do so in their own likeness. Managers are seen (by some) as aggressive, competitive and self-reliant. We have selected statements from women in our study who acknowledged having to pay a price for their positions in the man's world:

> One makes compromises – I hope I haven't made too many – when one is a woman working with a majority of men. This causes problems for women like myself. I certainly believe in devolved management. If you try to introduce that kind of management it does not meet the expectations of most men. They feel uncomfortable as most of their experiences have been with more hierarchical forms of management. They might interpret this as weakness at first. You have to compromise to meet male expectations to a certain degree in order to effect change.
> (Senior woman, Higher Education)

> It is very difficult in a position of management not to adopt a male model. In a sense you have to play them at their own game in order to get on. On the other hand you don't want to adopt a bad model of management, which I think many men operate, a style of management that doesn't get enough out of people because it doesn't offer them enough flexibility.
> (Head of a Teachers' Centre)

> Often women who become managers become male on the way and lose themselves. I have used the male way to get things done.
> (Retired Deputy Head)

> There are differences between women and men managers but most institutions operate according to male rules so influencing them is very difficult. Women who make it in macho institutions usually do so by pretending to be men which means they fit the clone description.
> (Senior Lecturer, Higher Education)

Several women in our study mentioned the difficulties of adopting the management style they preferred because the people they managed were demanding to be 'led'. A head of department said:

> I have always previously worked in departments where we have all worked together as a team. That's how I tried to manage the department at my present school, to work collectively, a feminist way of working. Instead I found I was working with people who wanted to be told exactly what to do. I couldn't understand this as I had never needed to be told what to do. I couldn't get working collectively off the ground. Departments at my school just don't run like that. I must have been mad to have stayed for so long. In meetings I tried to revolve chair and minute taking. I asked one woman to take minutes, she refused, saying that was my job.

A retired head said:

> As Head I made decisions in consultation with other colleagues, but they increasingly wanted decisions made for them as pressure of government reforms wore them out. They couldn't see the point of discussions when the government dictated so much.

One woman said of her line-manger:

> She works in a non-directive way, talks a lot to people as individuals, listens well, is warm and supportive. I admire her style, but other team members seemed to get frustrated by her unwillingness to take charge.

A Further Education lecturer was aware of the difficulties women faced, but regretted her experiences of women distancing themselves from former friends and colleagues when they gained more senior positions:

> It is difficult for them if superimposed on institutions with a male structure, difficult for them to change that. It will be interesting to see if institutions run by recently appointed women will be radically different. You have to operate with outside forces. You have to take on some of the trappings and the ways. I have observed how relationships between women change when some move up.

Many of the women in our study felt that the level of compromise they were making was acceptable. One college vice-principal believed that women should come to terms with their power, take it and use it to develop a feminist management style, empowering people rather than managing. She emphasized encouraging personal development in staff and the importance of demystifying skills like budget control. She had no time for what she described as 'mother-earth' feminists holding each other back and remaining in low status jobs. Becoming a senior lecturer had been difficult for her as previously she had seen herself as a 'champion of the workers'. It meant a change in function and identity, which she achieved through therapy and counselling. She now had a 'grown-up job' and she employed a psychotherapist to help the women in the college come to terms with their power.

A Media Resources Officer talked about the possible contradictions of women's fear of losing a sense of being 'part of a gang' by taking on more powerful positions and yet at the same time wanting power, though not power in the male sense. These aspects are further discussed in Chapter 6.

Carpenter (1989) describes the problems and compromises feminists make if they become administrators, or in a British context, a manager – a key area of our research project. She argues that feminists are unlikely to become administrators first and foremost for the money, or for the sense of power or prestige, but because they believe that they can make the institution more humane, more responsive, more feminist. In spite of their efforts they remain a very small minority within a patriarchal system, having to compromise their feminist principles every day. They are often expected by others to solve all the problems related to women and minorities in their institutions. Those who last are the ones who learn to pick their battles, to concede defeat and move on, to weigh their defeats against their victories and assess whether the price they have paid is too dear. She describes the dilemma women face:

> As individual feminist educators we can choose to remain in the ranks, where we can be most directly involved in the educational process and where we are called upon to make fewer compromises. Or we can become administrators in the hope that at best we can effect significant and structural change and at worst we can influence small scale monetary and policy decisions and present a feminist viewpoint in political debates; in exchange we agree to pay the price of compromise.
>
> (Carpenter, 1989, p. 44)

She argues that feminists should support feminist administrators by understanding the problems they face, though not necessarily agreeing with all their decisions.

> We who are like her but not like her, owe her a great deal. We owe her for the many small changes in our work lives and work environments, many of them changes we will never know she had a hand in creating. And we owe her for the sacrifices she has made in pursuit of the larger change which is our common goal.
>
> (Carpenter, 1989, p. 45)

Judi Marshall considered compromises that had to be made by women managers with a feminist or woman-centred approach. Her research focused on the experiences of women managers outside education but is relevant here because it makes the important distinction between female managers and feminist managers (Marshall, 1984).

In our study, we found that some women were clearly unhappy at the compromises that other women had made. A woman working in Further Education observed:

> There are some differences between women and male managers but I wish there were more. I get depressed by women managers imitating men.

A nursery teacher, with a small child, commented sceptically:

> I don't think there is a lot of difference between women and men managers, even women heads with children are not necessarily more supportive to teachers with young children.

This contradicts views expressed by several women in senior positions. Thus we see the same issue from two aspects.

Other women admitted to using male tactics because they felt that they were more effective and did not see any great contradiction in doing this:

> I am a manager who got promoted by the man's rules. I tend to reinforce those rules as I got promoted by them. However on the whole education is more co-operative than business. My role is about negotiating, advising and persuading. My one experience of a co-operative/feminist group was not so happy and in the end a line-manager relationship had to be established to rescue the situation.
>
> (Senior Inspector)

I am authoritarian. Women have to be tough. The reality is that the buck stops here and participation is an ideal. However, I do think that women managers are more open and receptive, they do care, whereas men tend to be manipulative, something that women are often accused of.

(Head of Department in Further Education)

Gareth Morgan (1986) states quite categorically that organizations are dominated by gender-related values and it therefore makes a great deal of difference whether you are a woman or a man:

As long as organisations are dominated by patriarchal values and structures the roles of women in organisations will always be played out in male terms . . . (The) real challenge facing women who want to succeed in the organisational world is to change the organisational values in the most fundamental way.

(Morgan, 1986, p. 212)

Organizations, he suggests, operate in ways that produce gender-related biases that are both overt, for example sexual harassment, and covert. He agrees with those feminists who have noted that organizations segment opportunities and job markets in ways that enable men to achieve positions of power and prestige more easily than women. He highlights the argument that the bureaucratic model tends to foster the rational, analytic and instrumental characteristics associated with maleness with a graphic description:

In the process it has created organisations that in more ways than one define a 'man's world,' where men, and the women who have entered the fray, joust and jostle for positions of dominance like stags contesting the leadership of their herd.

(Morgan, 1986, p. 211)

But even if women do 'enter the fray' and compromise, they are still women, the 'other sex' and will be judged as such. Research conducted in Canada (Sheppard, 1989) showed that women, in order to be taken seriously, have to 'manage' their sexuality and gender. Gender was usually seen in terms of barriers to women's participation; sexuality was viewed in relation to sexual harassment and control of sexuality. Maleness, because it is so embedded and taken for granted, is not seen as problematic. As we note too, women confront the dualism of being 'feminine' and 'businesslike' at the same time. Gender is seen as primarily a problem for women. The strategies that women use to deal with this conflict include styles of dress, language, relationships with others and 'blending in'.

For lesbians the problems are exacerbated as they must also deal with the complex process of managing discrediting information about themselves. In the man's world of organizations, women face boundaries that have no rules, and are likely to change depending on the male norms being employed. Sheppard uses the imagery of 'walking on a tightrope/walking on eggshells', noting that the small number of women in top positions gives them high visibility. Women who do not appear or act feminine enough may come to be seen as too masculine, a definition that may result in homophobia. And, no matter how well they manage their sexuality and gender, women's sexuality is always available as a means of control by covert or overt behaviours, from humiliation to violence.

Organizations, including schools, reproduce this '. . . life in a . . . heterosexual world in which men dominate and women learn to be compliant and subordinate to men' noted Stephen Ball (1987). For example, derogatory jokes and comments are one way of excluding. Sexual innuendo and even harassment are ways of controlling. Language and conversations within organizations often exclude black and white women and black men, who are in the minority in the management teams. Such talk is often about areas outside the experience of that organization's minority and therefore participation becomes difficult. One woman told us:

> I'm the only woman in the senior management team in an all-boys school. I often feel like a real fish out of water. Sport is so important – the major topic of conversation.

For this woman, social life at work is defined by male interests and experiences. Her position of isolation is constantly reinforced.

Figure 1.1

CHAPTER 2

Careers: Teaching – A Nice Job For A Nice Girl?

As most managers are men, so most teachers are women. In primary and secondary schools, 62 per cent of all teachers are women. Overall (that is, schools, Further and Higher Education), women make up more than half of the total teaching staff.

Sector	Women (%)
Primary	81
Secondary	47
Further Education	27
University	13

Source: DES Education Statistics for the UK 1990 (DES, 1991).

As these figures show, women predominate in the areas of teaching with lower status, where skills are perceived to be akin to caring and mothering. And within this, women's position in schools shows a gender bias. Despite the large number of women teachers in primary schools – four times the number of male teachers – men are disproportionately represented at head-teacher level. Currently, the existence of women Chief Education Officers (CEOs) is made much of but there are only 16 women in the total of 108 CEOs in England and Wales (Darking, 1991).

As tables 2.1, 2.2 and 2.3 show, men are disproportionately in higher-paid, higher status and management positions.

Table 2.1 Teachers by highest responsibility in secondary schools (percentages).

Highest responsibility:	Men		Women		Total	
	Full-time	*Part-time*	*Full-time*	*Part-time*	*Full-time*	*Part-time*
Head teacher	4	1	1	–	3	–
Deputy head	7	–	4	–	5	–
Head/deputy head of faculty or department	46	12	31	5	39	6
Head of year	9	2	9	–	9	1
Other responsibility[1]	14	15	17	5	15	6
No responsibilities	21	70	38	90	29	87
Total	100	100	100	100	100	100
All teachers (thousands)	103.0	3.6	88.4	26.0	191.3	29.6

– Less than 0.5
[1] Includes SEN of INSET coordination, or 'other significant management or organizational responsibility'
Source: DES (1991).

Table 2.2 Teachers by pay scale[1] (percentages)

	Men		Women		Total	
	Full-time	Part-time	Full-time	Part-time	Full-time	Part-time
Head teacher	4	1	1	–	3	–
Deputy head teacher	7	–	4	–	5	–
Main scale with:						
incentive allowance: E	6	2	2	–	4	–
D	21	7	8	–	15	1
C	2	1	2	–	2	–
B	26	10	22	1	24	2
A	3	4	4	1	4	1
no incentive allowance	31	63	57	91	43	87
Other scales[2]	–	13	1	7	1	7
Total	100	100	100	100	100	100
All teachers (thousands)	103.0	3.6	88.4	26.0	191.3	29.6

– Less than 0.5.
[1] Comparison with information from the Department's Database of Teacher Records indicates that junior teachers (i.e. main scale without an allowance) are slightly under-represented in the survey sample.
[2] Includes scales for unqualified teachers.
Source: DES (1991).

Table 2.3 Teachers by Burnham scale and sex in primary schools (percentages).

	Heads	Deputy heads	Scale 3[1]	Scale 2	Scale 1[2]	Total (thousands)
Men						
Full-time	32.0	21.0	11.9	25.7	9.4	32.1
Part-time	2.8	0.2	23.4	23.7	50.0	4.4
Women						
Full-time	7.5	8.5	7.3	37.1	39.6	127.5
Part-time	0.6	0.2	3.1	13.8	82.3	29.1
Total						
Full-time	12.4	11.0	8.2	34.8	33.5	159.6
Part-time	0.9	0.2	5.7	15.1	78.1	33.5

[1] Including Senior teacher and Scale 4.
[2] Including a small number of teachers not paid on Burnham scales.
Source: DES, (1991).

Often the 'feminization' of teaching has been blamed for women's relative lack of status and pay. Teaching children is associated with motherhood, marriage and the caring aspects of femininity. It is seen as an acceptable job for women, and as one that fits with women's other roles. Ironically, the marriage bar in existence in Britain before the Second World War excluded a large number of women from a profession in which they had been trained. The lifting of that barrier, as with others affecting women's careers, had more to do with demographic, political and socio-economic changes than with progressive thinking.

It should, however, be recognized that despite these limitations teaching is relatively well paid compared with other paid professional 'women's work', such as nursing, social work and librarianship. It also has, relative to these jobs, reasonable potential of individual career advancement.

But women teachers, whether they remain rooted in the classroom or whether they decide to move into middle or higher management, do not follow a straightforward career path paralleling that of their male colleagues. The structure of the profession is pyramidical. The only way to substantially increase pay and status is to move into the apex of that pyramid. For those women in education who do decide that they want to move up, there is the so-called 'glass ceiling', the invisible barrier to achievement; the point at which women watch younger men in grey suits gain positions of power. Whether this barrier is created by male assumptions of their right to advancement or female reticence and non-aggressive attitudes remains moot. On the one hand, 'It's not so much that these young men queue-jump; it's that they are in a different queue' (Segerman Peck, 1991). On the other:

> We didn't think of a career structure. You waited to be asked. We belong to a group of people who did our best and hoped it would be recognized and an offer would be made.
>
> (Grant 1989b, p. 39)

The relatively small number of women in senior positions and the nature of their posts has been noted by many. Torrington and Weightman include a chapter on women in management in their book *The Reality of School Management* (1989). The authors point out that they did not specifically set out to study the role of women but were struck by two factors; first that there were a small number of women in senior posts and second that women were doing different kinds of work from men. Their investigation analysed the posts for all teachers above Scale 3 (Standard National Scale plus C allowance) in 24 schools. They found that while men were heads of faculty, heads of sixth form, deputy heads and head teachers, women were heads of year, heads of upper and lower school and heads of special education. Only two women were not in pastoral posts. The posts held by men were fairly discrete activities whereas the posts held by women required across-school liaison. Men tended to have high profile, straightforward jobs with roles that were easily understood and accepted – the male post-holder is perceived as a manager, doing managerial work. Women's jobs, however, involved cross-school skills and were not as easily understood by others. As a result, these women were not seen as managers. One negative effect of this showed in their applications for promotion, where it was difficult for them to gain recognition as senior managers.

While these research findings differ somewhat from our own, as the majority of women in our study were in senior but not specifically pastoral positions, we did hear that:

> I've applied for quite a lot of senior management positions in the past year. I get short-listed for some but at the interview it seems to me that they are looking for someone with a straight manage-ment background. A chap. The kind of skills which I know are

transferable aren't considered right. As a teacher, a woman, a mother, I've been managing – in both senses of the word – all my life. Now I feel I need a MBA to prove it!

(Teacher)

Women who do get through the glass ceiling continue to experience inequality. Mortimore and Mortimore (1991), in a recent publication on the experiences of secondary heads, record the comments of seven heads on their perceptions of headship. One of the three women in their study commented specifically on the sexism she faced. A black headteacher commented on the racism and sexism she encountered:

I had to work hard – doubly hard to prove I was a good head, a good, black headteacher; a good, black, female headteacher. I felt I was in a glass cage. I felt very lonely.

(Mortimore and Mortimore, 1991, p. 81)

The authors describe the prevailing image of a white, middle class headmaster and recommend counteracting it with successful role models.

Many of the women in our study *were* these successful role models. They were not representative of the teaching profession as a whole, where women predominate in the main professional grades and in part-time work; they were 'high up', well paid and therefore relatively powerful. Several women in senior positions discussed role models, stressing their own personal impact and influence on children, students and staff. Although role models present a challenge they are, alone, not enough to end a pattern of male and white dominance – as noted earlier, the hierarchical system protects itself and ensures its perpetuation.

Figure 2.1

Promotion: myths and realities

Some literature explains women's career prospects in terms of women's deficiency and inability to accept the challenge of promotion. But several recent studies have attempted to find a different explanation for women's exclusion from powerful positions in education. Two studies, one by Davidson (1985) and one by Warwickshire County Council (1989), used interviews and found that reality does not match myth. The Warwickshire study identifies some of the assumptions about women teachers:

- they are under-qualified;
- they are not interested in furthering their careers;
- they prioritize their children to the detriment of their jobs;
- they take career breaks and lose impetus;
- they are tied to a spouse's career;
- they cannot give time outside the school day because family commitments take priority;
- only single women progress well.

The study then provides evidence from teachers in the county refuting these broad assumptions (Warwickshire County Council, 1989, p. 4). Both studies found that women and men are equally interested in promotion, although women are more aware of and subject to discrimination. They identified a lack of training and experience as the most significant factors affecting women's chances of promotion. We believe that even when training is available, the self-perpetuating nature of the organization, its ethos and structures, still limit women's chances of promotion. We heard this:

> They said I wasn't quite what they were looking for [in an interview for deputy head]. I'm in my forties; with an MA in education and a diploma in educational management. I've been on numerous management courses and have had the experience of being a senior teacher. The job went to a smart young chap who had been an HoD for three years and had a BA. He was in exactly the same mould as the head!
>
> (Senior teacher)

The two studies mentioned above refute the myth that women are poorly qualified. Similarly, Mary Lyn Jones (1990) found, in her study of a Welsh LEA, that 'women teachers were the best and men head teachers the worst qualified' (p. 12), yet a large number of women and only one man in her sample were on Scale 1 (Standard National Scale).

Other assumptions, as listed from the Warwickshire study, make misleading generalizations, e.g. that career breaks lead to loss of impetus. Although some women do take career breaks, their success on returning to work is hindered by external factors, including other people's prejudices. The percentage of women taking career breaks to have children is lower than generally assumed. An ILEA study of London and Birmingham school teachers recorded that 21 per cent in Birmingham, and only 11 per cent in London, took breaks for this reason. However, both men and women take breaks to further their career. The phenomenon of men who take career breaks to take care of their children is virtually unknown.

Some assumptions, e.g. prioritizing children, can be turned on their heads and viewed positively. This from our study:

> I'd worry about myself if I got into that trap of seeing my job as terribly important – more important than my children. I'm really committed and I enjoy my job but it's not in the same league as my children. I'm a strong feminist and fight for our rights to have children and jobs – but I'm not willing to deny the joy I get from being a mother. To me, it is a question of my values and philosophy. I think I'm a better teacher and manager *for* having a complex, rounded life.
>
> (Senior teacher)
>
> Neglecting children in favour of your career had always been what men have traditionally done. I know that's tied up with expectations placed on men by society and incorporated into our laws – the family wage and all that. But I don't want to take on these macho attitudes and attributes. My children aren't a hobby.
>
> (Teacher)

The combination of teaching/marriage/parenthood have different effects on the relative careers of women and men. For men it may provide an incentive for promotion while for women the opposite may be true. A study of 24 education managers in Scotland by Elizabeth Gerver and Lesley Hart as reported in Darking (1991) found that women had been appointed to senior posts later than their male counterpart regardless of their career breaks. Fewer than half had children – often the result of a stark choice between career and family.

Figure 2.2

The overwhelming responsibility placed on mothers and the lack of support with childcare in this society represents a form of oppression – we discuss this further in Chapter 3. The mothers in our study talked and wrote about their children at length. The following examples, selected because they were typical of many, indicate that many mothers recognize anxiety and guilt in combining the role of carer with their career:

> The decision to remain at work with small children involves juggling responsibilities.
>
> There is constant guilt about children and the third job after work and home, of organizing the children.
>
> Putting your kids first definitely hinders your career. Difficult choices have to be made.
>
> Having a young child limits the amount of commitment that can be made – no job requiring evening, weekends or long hours. It

makes it impossible to give as much as is required in the 1990's and puts up obstacles to applying for/securing certain jobs.

Having children is usually detrimental to a woman's career. The guilt and having to make choices that mean personal compromise and sacrifice.

There is always anxiety about being a working mother no matter how old they are.

Having children has had a profound influence on my career. At times I have had to forgo applying for promotion.

Children had a cataclysmic effect on my career. We – mothers – juggle our lives and make sacrifices.

I rush from one set of responsibilities to another.

While we do not wish to suggest it is easy to combine motherhood with careers, it can be a positive choice to do both. Carol Adams writes in the *Times Educational Supplement* in response to an article on women Chief Education Officers:

I would like to take the opportunity to redress the balance by confirming that it is not only perfectly feasible to combine a chief education officer's job with having young children – 80-hour week, weekend work and all, but there are positive professional advantages in being a parent.

Career ambition

Countering the mythology is evidence that some women are 'career ambitious'. A lecturer in Further Education in our own study encapsulated this saying:

I'm going to be a college principal by the time I'm forty. That's my ambition – and I'm not going to let the racism and sexism of the system block me.

Julia Evetts surveyed career-ambitious women in education. Her data came initially from life-history interviews with 15 married women who were heads of infant or primary schools. Like us, Evetts is careful to contextualize her research. The women in her first study all sought headships in the 1960s or 1970s – a time very different from the 1980s and 1990s. As has been said before, the 1960s were an era of optimism. The post-War birth rate meant a huge expansion of schools. Clearly, teachers' careers are influenced by economic, social and political factors external to the profession.

Evetts warns that the words 'career' and 'ambition' need to be used with caution. Most of the women in her studies found the word 'ambition' derogatory. The language itself, with implications of competitiveness and aggression, present a barrier to many women. We found this too, observing that women disliked using the word 'power' because of its connotations, preferring words like 'influence'. Commonly, power was perceived in our study in hierarchical, linear terms. '. . . the higher up you are, the more responsibility you should take, the more powerful you are and the more you get paid' said a teacher.

Rosemary Grant is one of several who note that the concept of career ambition is irrelevant to most women as it is out of step with their life-styles. Women actively reject such notions as part of a male concept of career, which conflicts with their preferred allegiance to people-centred values, particularly in relation to women's rejection of male-defined power, the subject of Chapter 6. Career orientation based on a strong desire for advancement fits a career model, a clear path with defined steps leading towards a final target – a male model (built on men's experiences), which ignores the realities of women's lives. The majority of women in our study viewed their careers more holistically rather than within the 'single-minded' male stereotype, as the quotes from the senior teacher and teacher used earlier exemplify.

Getting into education

We asked the women in our research how they got into education. We also asked them how they would describe their career pattern – whether it was 'drift', plan or luck. The overwhelming majority said that their entry into education as a career was by drift or luck. The influence of families was often noted. Some were encouraged by parents who were either teachers themselves or who saw teaching as a good job for girls. We have already mentioned teaching as a way of combining motherhood, marriage and a career. Our research findings on career choice seem to be in line with others. Hart (1989) interviewed heads and deputy heads on their career aspirations. All the women in her research felt that they had achieved their positions more by good luck than good management. Only one had a career plan. All felt that they had to make a choice between career and family – unlike men. Similarly, Rosemary Grant (1989b) found that women were unlikely to begin teaching with a definite career plan and that their careers were shaped by developments in their personal lives. Women in Gerver and Hart's study, too, thought that luck had influenced their careers, rather than planning. They noted that prejudice played a part too – and many had to change employers to find more positive attitudes towards women.

These phrases were said or written by women in our study:

- I had lots of luck and my career was totally unplanned;
- I have always been in the right place at the right time. Lucky!
- I drifted into a PGCE;
- I had no particular plan, just good luck;
- I kind of drifted into teaching;
- It – my career – has been entirely haphazard and accidental;
- Getting into teaching and now management – it has been quite definitely drift and luck . . .
- I did drift for 18 years then I made some attempt to work out a career plan. But my entry into education was arbitrary. I had no plan but considered myself particularly lucky. I am a lucky drifter;
- It's been luck – no career plan. Having started out with teaching because I couldn't think what else to do, I kept coming back to it;
- My career was drift, then luck, and now (finally) planning.

A number of women entered education because it fitted in with their domestic arrangements and being mothers. Examples included:

- I went into teaching after marriage;
- Teaching fits in with motherhood and being a wife;
- I needed a job that fitted in with caring for my young children – teaching was an obvious answer.

Some were given careers advice:

- My careers teacher suggested teaching – 'you're a woman and doing English therefore you ought to teach';
- I was told to either do social work or teaching.

Parents were also influential in career choice for some women:

- My parents were teachers. A 'safe' qualification;
- My parents were teachers and I was expected to be one too;
- Parental pressure; parental/grandparental example – all teachers;
- My parents saw entering teaching as a way for me to get on and to become middle class.

A few women went in to teaching as a 'second choice':

- I went into teacher training because I couldn't get into university;
- I drifted into education. I wanted to go to university but my grades weren't good enough;
- I wanted to do Sociology at university but couldn't get in so I went to teacher training college instead.

Some women in our study, many of whom had attained positions of power, appeared to be relatively powerless in choosing their careers. However, we did find a minority of women who consciously and positively chose education as their career. Most of these women were in their late thirties and forties and their decisions to enter teaching should be seen within the context of the 1960s and 1970s in Britain. Class struggle and the belief that education could change the status quo bringing about a more egalitarian society, as reflected in the move to comprehensive schooling, had an impact on an individual's choices and indicated their political motivation and perspectives:

- I had a strong commitment to education as a librarian rather than as a teacher;
- I wanted to do something useful. I did choose and plan carefully;
- I planned my teaching experience, was invited to join the INSET (Inservice training of teachers) team, and planned my inspectorate career;

- Getting into education was a conscious choice – I always wanted to teach;
- For me entering teaching was an ideological decision. I saw it as a possible way to change society for the better.

Education was much more politically acceptable than business or industry.

Mentors

One question we asked in our study was about mentors. Women had different views of what a mentor was. For many, the concept of a mentor was quite alien and the reality unknown. Although they did not use the word mentor several paid tribute to men who had helped them. For example:

I had a lot of support and encouragement from my male Head of Department – not a grey-suited one. He helped me a lot in my first years of teaching. He took an explicit interest in me.

(Head)

My first head of house was very supportive, fatherly, really. He taught me things that disciplined me as a teacher – like cleaning the board.

(Teacher)

There was some confusion around the word itself. One woman thought that her biggest driving force was the desire to please and the fear of letting anyone down – 'them' being those who encouraged her to seek promotion. While specifically asked about mentors, the women talked about friendship from other women, encouragement from men and support in their early days of teaching. One woman made the distinctions, saying she had 'Lots of support, some mentoring and some role models and friendships'. Another woman talked with gratitude about a woman in her first school who had told her that:

I had a lot of potential and would make a good Head of Department. Since then, I have seen how useful it is to have the continuing support of a good manager – and try to be one myself.

(Head of Department)

One way to get to the top is with the support of mentors and networks. Men are frequently in a position to be mentors. Unfortunately for women, mentors tend to chose protégés who are like themselves, so men chose men. Furthermore, when men create networks, these often exclude women – the 'locker-room syndrome'.

In conclusion, we saw in our study that some women were ambitious and wanted to move through the glass ceiling into positions of power whilst others rejected this pursuit. Just as with all other aspects of women's lives, career decisions and experiences are diverse. We saw a complex and shifting interplay of personal, political and professional choices, opportunities and constraints.

CHAPTER 3

Feminism: Managing Through A Different Lens

Feminism is taught through process as well as formal content. To reflect feminist values in teaching is to teach progressively, democratically, and with feeling. Such teaching rejects what Paulo Freire calls the 'banking system of education', a system that assumes that one person with greater power and wisdom has the knowledge to dispense to others. Feminist education implies that we enter into a dialogue with other students, meeting them as human beings, and learning with them in community.

(Schniedewind, 1983, p. 271)

We have tried to make the connections between feminist education, feminist management and feminist methodology. In this chapter we discuss feminism under headings chosen in an attempt to keep theory close to the research and data. The headings are:

- personal perspectives
- women and oppression
- theory and practice

We decided not to use the more usual approach of discussing feminism in discrete theoretical traditions – Marxist feminism, liberal feminism, radical feminism, essentialist feminism, etc., for two reasons. First, there is a wealth of literature documenting various feminisms. (Rosemary Tong's *Feminist Thought: A Comprehensive Introduction* (1989) was one book we found useful with its description of, and debate on, feminisms.) Second, classification and categorization is problematic and, we felt, undesirable, when applied to people. But we do identify and discuss feminist traditions and perspectives where relevant.

Few women stated that they were rigidly within any one particular tradition of feminism and very few labelled themselves saying, for example, 'I am a radical feminist'. Many women seemed reluctant to label themselves. However, there was identification and acknowledgement, particularly from some of the black and ethnic minority women and lesbians in our study, of aspects of feminism that had been important in women's history as well as in women's own lives. The distinction between 'labelling' and self-identification is worth exploring briefly. Labelling, when externally imposed, can have negative connotations and be seen as limiting. It implies myths and stereotypes, taking it beyond neutral categorization. Identification, on the other hand, is positive and empowering. It implies analysis and a wish to be linked with some aspects of an identifiable group. One woman said:

> I don't like it when people label me as a Jew and a lesbian. It is usually said as an insult. But I identify myself positively as a Jewish lesbian with others.

Each of us identified ourselves as feminists. We recognized and discussed the difficulty and sometimes absurdity of placing and fixing ourselves in a single category as we 'use' different kinds of feminism in different social situations. As women attempting to practise feminism in our working and personal lives, we were conscious of these contradictions. For example, we recognized and discussed compromises we made in our employment situations in education where we have to operate as equal opportunities/liberal feminists while in our private lives some of us were and are more radical or socialist. It is important to recognize that we are not static – the context in which we are living and working affects us. We continue to grow and develop, hopefully.

In the original project, we did not ascribe to any one feminist theory or perspective. We recognized eclecticisms as well as diversity within our approaches, and so drew on many and various aspects of both theory and practice. This is not to imply that the four of us who conducted the research shared an identical view of feminism or that we all agreed about the nature and source of male power. However, our collective understanding is that feminism is a political commitment to change – whether that is on the streets, in the home, the workplace or in our relationships. For each of us, feminism places women at the centre, and gives us ways of analysing, understanding and relating to the world.

We used a feminist methodology, which included group activity and collective contribution, attempting to move away from androcentric ways of working that are often inherent in educational management and research generally. Feminism as an issue in research is not, of course, a new and undocumented area. The dissatisfaction and therefore a break with 'tradition' underlies the work of many feminists. For example:

> We have tried to make it clear that the grounds on which we've said what we have aren't those of 'scholarship' or 'correctness' but feelings and experience.
>
> (Stanley and Wise, 1983, p. 177)

But this is not always easy! Because of our own training and conditioning, we had to check continually that we were not falling into a patriarchal way of working, unquestioningly replicating male academia – a problem that occurred on all levels, including language use and structure. Aspects of feminist writing and structure were part of our consciousness throughout the preparation of the original research project, continuing into our current project – this book. Alternatives have been a subject of feminist concern and research for years. To break with patriarchal patterns, 'a woman must be a thief of language' (Ostriker, 1987) and write 'in a different voice' (Gilligan, 1982) because:

> Words, sentences, writing styles, ways of presenting arguments, arguments themselves, criticism . . . all these are part and parcel of masculinist culture. They are among the artifacts of sexism and their use structures our experience before we can even begin to examine it, because they provide us with how we think as well as how we write.
>
> (Stanley and Wise, 1983, p. 185)

Personal perspectives

Dale Spender writes personally in *What is Feminism?* disclosing that her early experience of sisterhood was via her sense of privilege at having a (biological) sister. She recognizes her first experience of sisterhood as an important forerunner to her later commitment to the political sisterhood of feminism and explains that

My choice of feminism was a logical one, a deliberate decision to improve the quality of my life. I selected feminism as a way of life, as a value system and as a means of explaining the world and my place within it.

(Spender, 1987, p. 215)

She considers feminism to be based on a 'better' set of assumptions than any other world view; to be a fairer way of viewing and organizing the world. The challenge for feminism is to be able to include the diversity of human experience. Both these points were important to many of the women in our survey, as examples will show.

Our research

Most of the women in our study stated that they were feminists, although this clearly meant different things to different women. The identification as feminists is not surprising as many of the women were our friends, colleagues or acquaintances, and/or women who had at some time been involved in equal opportunities work. In addition, placing advertisements in *Spare Rib* and *The Guardian* 'Women's page' meant that we targeted women who might define themselves as feminists.

In asking women whether they were feminists and what feminism meant to them we all noticed that these questions were frequently met with a long pause. Responses in the interviews were thoughtful and a number of women decided to return to these questions later in the interview. We could see from the written responses that some of the women had returned to the question; in several instances women had used different pens or made additions or alterations. There were contradictions and ambiguities within individual replies. Our findings on the issue of identification with feminism are similar to those in other studies, for example, Simeone's study of twenty women in higher education. Of these women, nine identified themselves as feminists without qualification; eight had some reservations or ambivalence; three were '. . . certain that they weren't feminist, [but] one seemed to be leaning somewhat in that direction' (Simeone, 1987, p. 97).

We have presented something of the range of responses we received, showing differences as well as similarities between women's views:

It feels like I have always been a feminist but I haven't always had the words for it. It comes from very deep within. It is of deep spiritual significance as well as political.

(Head of Department)

Yes, I am a feminist. It means a different way of seeing and experiencing the world from the dominant male model we are asked to accept as normal and valuing those differences.

(Ex-deputy Head)

Yes, I am a feminist. Proudly. Feminism means a sense of solidarity, liking myself and making it easier for women to come together. Understanding power – especially male power. Feminism has given me and all women strength in order to understand our own power. Feminism humanizes institutions and makes the workplace better for everyone.

(Media Resources Officer)

Several women wrote or said that they no longer felt the need for feminism. In a written response, one woman used the term post-feminism, describing herself as such (tentatively, with a series of question-marks) while 'recognizing the continuing need to change men and my wish to support other women'. Some women regarded themselves as feminists, but no longer active or informed.

I am a lapsed radical feminist, lapsed because I don't have the time to do what I did in the past.

(Inspector)

In this woman's view, feminism associates solely with activism outside of the home and interpersonal relations. Does this divorce the personal from the political? We wondered whether this ignores women's struggles when they live in an intimate relationship in a household with others.

A contrasting view of feminism as an individual issue, rather than a political one, was occasionally expressed. 'No, I'm not a feminist. My father taught me that I was able to do anything from an early age' wrote an inspector, and a senior teacher remarked that she did not need feminism as she had a very supportive husband. This minority of women in our study apparently regard feminism quite differently from those who commented on feminism as a world view leading to change and whose base line is an understanding of patriarchy.

One woman expressed this view:

No, I'm not a feminist. I accept that men and women are different and don't try to be a man. (This woman responded to one of our advertisements; she addressed us as 'Dear Sirs')

(Ex-acting Head)

A few women were ambivalent about their own identification as feminists. A senior teacher in Further Education described herself as a liberated woman, and said she was unsure of the meaning of feminism. A senior librarian replied in similar terms, writing:

I am strongly pro-women but feel I lack the knowledge and perceptions of the political dimension of women's experience to claim the title feminist.

Ex-feminists; post-feminists; women who recognized the limitations of white, middle-class feminism; women who disliked the connotations of the word 'feminism' while holding a woman-centred perspective – our study revealed a wide range of views.

Although they knew that we four were feminists engaged in feminist research, three women espoused violently anti-feminist views while still making helpful and friendly contributions to our project. Perhaps this reflects a perception of the interviews as a safe environment in which women felt able to express themselves without fear of censure, as mentioned in Chapter 4. Clearly, it is important that views contrary to the researchers' can be expressed – otherwise the research itself is nothing more than a self-fulfilling (and smug) exercise. We valued people being open and honest and not giving a response to please us.

We believe there were elements of homophobia underlying a few of the statements we heard and read on feminism.

Feminism? I don't know what it means. I'm a very feminine woman. I like being a woman. Wearing nice clothes, looking nice. I like men very much. Feminists don't want to be seen as women and they do their gender harm trying to look like blokes. I had a friend, a radical feminist who used to wear dungarees and boots, and she had really cropped hair. Now, she power dresses and looks terrific. The women's movement has moved on.

(Ex-senior Teacher)

One woman seemed bluntly anti-lesbian in her answer to 'are you a feminist?'

Yes – defensively. I object to the stereotype feminist – the bra-burner and lesbian. I want to be my own feminist.

(Senior Adviser)

Despite our previous comment on the value of honest response it was not easy to avoid questioning and challenging views.

Ourselves

The four sections that follow were written individually and illustrate our different approaches and styles. Like the contributions from women in our research, ours are 'snapshots' located at a particular time in our lives. They are shortened and edited versions of items written in May 1990.

Jenny

> Within feminism I found respect for female experience. What women do, say and think is taken as the foundation on which to base concepts and models of the world . . . Western society is essentially a patriarchy in which men hold authority and women are oppressed or ignored. These inequalities are reflected in our social institutions, in the distribution of work, in the pattern of interpersonal relationships and the language through which we express and transmit our culture.
>
> (Marshall, 1984, p. 44)

This quotation, in many ways, represents my interpretation of feminism, an interpretation that I have only reached quite recently (within the last five years).

I was encouraged by my parents not to build my life around being a wife and mother and not to let myself be limited by my sex. My girls' grammar school perpetuated the idea that girls could do anything they wanted; all they needed were the right qualifications. My first glimpse of harsh reality was at fifteen when I took a holiday job in a local biscuit factory. I was horrified to discover that the women earned two-thirds of the men's wage for doing exactly the same job. Following this experience I worked even harder for my A levels in the misguided belief that a university degree would protect me from sexual discrimination. I suppose I would describe myself at that stage as a liberal feminist (my definition now, not one I would have used then). I read Betty Friedan's *The Feminine Mystique* soon after it came out, lent to me by a teacher at school, which helped to confirm my belief that the road to liberation consisted of becoming an honorary man.

At university I joined a spectrum of socialist organizations but never felt able to identify fully with any of their interpretations of the world . . . I became involved in the women's movement in 1969 but was not, looking back on it, woman-centred. I considered class more important than sex, not regarding women's struggle as really important. Although I read all the 'right' books, I had little affinity for women. Feminism, for me, at that stage, was almost an intellectual exercise; it did not really touch my life or my relationships. One exception to this was Firestone's *The Dialectic of Sex*. It was her negative assessment of biological motherhood that was mainly responsible for my decision not to have children. However, again I was attempting to avoid oppression as a woman by avoiding being like a woman. I spent (wasted) too many years trying to beat men at their own game, thinking that the world of men was more exciting than the world of women. Everything would be all right 'come the revolution'. I still felt that being an honorary man would help me escape oppression as a woman.

Only comparatively recently have I come to appreciate the energy and value of women. In the past, in trying to avoid discrimination as a woman, I buried my female side and am only just finding it again.

Now my feminism is a way of life; an intrinsic part of me. It is to do with valuing women, valuing myself as a woman, supporting and empowering other women, valuing women's power, achievements, culture, women's frequently unrecognized contribution to the world. It also means appreciating that these beliefs will bring me into conflict with most men and also many women and that confronting patriarchy will be a daily occurrence from which there is no escape apart from abandoning my beliefs.

However, my view isn't a biologically deterministic one. I think men can and do change, though many choose not to.

I would find it difficult to fit myself into any particular category such as a liberal, Marxist, Socialist, radical, psychoanalytic, existential or post-modern feminist. I agree with radical feminists that the patriarchal system oppresses women, that it is not only legal and political structures that must be overturned but social and cultural institutions as well. I also think class is important, but not more important than gender. If I had to categorize myself it would probably be as a socialist feminist using Tong's (1989) definition. She describes socialist feminism as 'the confluence of Marxist, radical and more arguably psychoanalytic streams of thought.'

I disagree with Freud's interpretation of female sexuality and what I consider to be his biological determinism. However, I do believe that past experiences, including early childhood experiences, have an effect on us, but as only one in a number of factors. Whilst I find less of relevance in Freudian theory than does Mitchell (1971, 1974) I would agree with her that women's condition is determined by a number of factors. These include women's inner world or psyche, as well as the structures of production, reproduction, sexuality and the socialization of children. It is necessary for our inner as well as our outer world to be transformed. Political reforms alone will not liberate us from the thoughts absorbed and internalized from patriarchy. We need to fight our oppression on a number of different levels. I believe that political action will be most successful when it combines our ideas and experiences with the feelings and emotional energy we can tap through women's therapy groups and other facets of the growth movement. We are most powerful when we have both a political analysis and an understanding of our innermost feelings.

However, I remain uncertain that fitting myself, or other women into a category is at all useful. I am aware that as a white woman my perspective of feminism is different from that of a black woman. I am also aware that white women, in attempting to define feminism, have often completely ignored the experiences of black women. My feminism, and the understanding of my oppression, has developed throughout my life and, I hope, will continue to do so. It has developed organically, as a result of various experiences, from being with, talking to and working with other women. Reading feminist theory has helped me explain and understand my experiences and place them within a context. The different strands of thought within this provide useful alternative ways of looking at complex situations. To use these different strands to pigeon-hole women, to narrow down the debate to making a choice of label rather than opening it up, is highly divisive and does nothing to help women develop a deeper understanding of their situation.

I would agree with Tong when she writes:

> As bad as it is for a woman to be bullied into submission by a patriarch's unitary truth, it is even worse for her to be judged not a real feminist by a matriarch's unitary truth . . .
>
> (Tong, 1989, p. 236)

. . . What I treasure most about feminist thought, is that although it has a beginning it has no predetermined end, feminist thought permits each woman to think her own thoughts. Apparently, not the truth, but the truths are setting women free.

(Tong, 1989, p. 238)

Sue

Feminism means, to me, a way to perceive the world and operate in it. It is 'another' way of living and 'another' way of being. But I don't think of feminism as a static monolith – on the contrary it is the fluidity and complexity that appeals to me. I believe it is healthy and realistic. Its starting points, viewpoints and definitions are on a scale I feel at home with. I believe all situations, including the political and economic ones of this time, could be very different if women were in there, not as tokens or problems, but as half the world.

I remember Dale Spender saying that she looked forward to the day when strength was defined in female terms, not male. She talked about her Utopia – a place of collaborative, collective enterprise without competition. Perhaps this would be rather like Marge Piercy's in *Woman on the Edge of Time*. I too have a Utopian fantasy. So there are (at least) two feminisms for me. The one I live daily and the one I dream about. The one I dream about is the one where it all stops being 'another' way, where the many feminisms becomes *the* ways.

I found that women's comments in the interviews stimulated my own analysis of feminism. Often, I agreed; occasionally, I disagreed with the views expressed. I found it useful to consider my reaction and use contrast and criticism here – I have grown up in a male-defined world. For example, a woman told me:

> I was lucky – my partner is very supportive and he always had been so I didn't need feminism. And we were part of the 60s – men and women and liberation . . .

I know what she means about the 1960s, but I think her perception of feminism is limited and so sad. It implies that feminism is (just) a support system – something some women have (implied, too) until they find a Good Man. My own notion of feminism is that it is about support and friendship – yes – and that being able to establish and maintain responsible, reciprocal relationships with women and potentially, with men, is important. But it is also about external politics. Does a happy heterosexual relationship mean one does not 'need' to fight for the liberation of women? Does the fact that one was alive and kicking hard in the 1960s mean one has done one's bit in the struggle? I have some friends who are evidence that the answers to both must be 'No'.

Another comment depressed and bothered me:

> If feminism means you hate men, really radical [feminism], then no I'm not [a feminist] because I think kids need men as well as women . . .

Hating male exploitation and male competition does not mean – to me – necessarily the same thing as hating men. The stereotype of the man-hating feminist completely ignores the misogyny I see and experience. Substituting one form of oppression for another is no answer, and many of the women I interviewed for this project were clear that feminist alternatives have nothing to do with role-reversal.

On a positive note, then:

> Feminism means taking my womanhood seriously.

It means, too, not allowing anyone to rubbish womanhood. I particularly like Alice Walker's use of the word 'Womanist'.

What kind of feminist am I? I find classification problematic (ironic for a librarian). Attempting classification of women into groups of feminists confuses rather that clarifies the issues for me, and I am wary of over-simplification. Yet I have described myself as a radical feminist who usually (almost always) operates as a liberal feminist because I earn my money within a system that seems to find me fairly unacceptable even so. As I read more, I find myself beguiled by some post-modernist and essentialist feminist ideas. I always describe myself as a feminist and have ever since I learned the word. I remember reading Germaine Greer's *The Female Eunuch* in 1970 and being excited partly by the new ideas; partly by the familiarity and sense of recognition.

I like to think that I have been a feminist all my life. Like Dale Spender, my relationship with my own sister is central to my feminism. And my best childhood and teenage memories relate to friendships with other girls. My enormous pleasure in the company of my friends continues. Paralleling the importance of friendship from and of women are books – and I am indebted forever to feminist writers – academics, philosophers, poets and especially novelists.

I believe that the way we are working on the dissertation is feminism in a 1990s context – strong, positive, realistic and pragmatic. I think it has political implications that we should not allow to be belittled and trivialized. I was amazed at the generosity, openness and trust of the women I interviewed. I was knocked out by the speed with which we made contact and by the depth of that contact. Now that too is feminism/sisterhood/great.

Mary

Feminism for me is part of the way I live, work, am in the world. It is part of my very being as a woman. I cannot remember a time when I was not a feminist, although I haven't always had the words or language to give it a name.

This element of my feminism, being part of my very being, is echoed by some of the women we have interviewed who also felt that they didn't always have the words to express their feelings and even now talk about the difficulties of explaining something that is so much a part of the way they live their lives. Because it is so much a part of my woman-ness it is always there. The ways that I relate to other women, the assumptions that I make, the centrality of feminism and gender to my work, both the theory and the practice, and what I consider to be important in my life.

I could quote any number of women who have written about feminism in its various forms that would articulate some of my own views. The difficulty would be who to leave out – this would undoubtedly say more about my view of feminism than anything else. The books, new and old, fiction and non-fiction that continue to have an impact. The women I have met as I have journeyed through life that have influenced me (and the occasional man). The damage done to these by the patriarchal, class, ableist, racist, ageist, homophobic society in which I live and work and of which I am a product. The lovers, friends and colleagues who have influenced my life.

In the end, though, like most women, I take the elements from the various feminisms and fashion them into my own theory of the world. A theory that is constantly changing, affected by my practice as I try out different ways of being in the world. A world that I hope has a future and one in which women and feminism are an integral part. A world with a vision of the possibility of it being a better place for everyone. Feminism is then about the continuing challenge it has to offer, the strength and support that it has and continues to give me, about different ways of seeing the world although not necessarily the one true way. The possibilities of co-operation, collaboration and sharing that are always present when I am with women that I share a common vision with. The thrill and excitement of meeting others who share my commitment to feminism and its radical political potential.

Anne
I identified strongly with the women I interviewed who expressed guilt about their feminism. As a feminist I frequently feel guilty – I think I should be more active, more vocal, and much less compromising in my work situation. In the past three years, through my association with the women on this Open University course, my feminism has developed and strengthened. I am much more sure of my feminism and more able to analyse my work and personal life.

I came quite late to feminism, as a mature student teacher. I had married young and worked in the civil service with no contact whatsoever with feminists. It took me many years to accept feminism as I felt threatened by the middle-class nature of feminist groups and the slightly chaotic nature of the feminist organizations I had contact with. My three years spent at college doing a BEd gave me the opportunity to meet other women and to read widely. I finished the course in 1982 with clear ideas on race, class and gender and with the high hopes that I was going to be a 'good' teacher. I still had the vague feeling that 'the feminists' were meeting somewhere and I had still not found the venue!

My first year of teaching knocked me sideways, exhausted me and dented my faith in equal opportunities. There was no time for anything else other than work and my daughter – by this time I had become a single parent. It was a struggle to keep going and again I felt isolated, as there were few feminists on the staff of my first school. It took me several years to get to the point where I could put my feminism into practice. The feeling of always going against the grain became less exhausting and more exciting as I developed confidence and competence as a teacher.

My theoretical perspective on feminism is many stages beyond, or removed from, what I actually do at work and with my home life. I believe in women and socialism and in the fundamental right of each person to achieve and have pleasure in life. As a white woman I cannot assume an understanding of all oppressed groups but I can attempt a way of life that does not oppress others. My starting point is that women are consistently exploited through the family and all other institutions. I think it is important for women, however painful, to take positions of power and create better systems for other women. My theory is that powerful women with a feminist perspective can and do make a difference in organizations.

There are many aspects of feminism and sisterhood that I have yet to explore.

Women and oppression

I have learned that oppression and the intolerance of difference come in all shapes and sizes and colors and sexualities; and that among those of us who share the goals of liberation and a workable future for our children, there can be no hierarchy of oppression . . . I cannot afford to choose between the fronts upon which I must battle these forces of discrimination, where ever they appear to destroy me.

(Lorde, 1983, p. 3)

Many women in our research articulated or wrote on the intimate relationship between different forms of oppression at personal, political and professional levels. Several women revealed that their own focus was on one particular form. Several described connections between race, class, sex and sexuality. A woman who defined herself as a black socialist feminist made it clear to the interviewer that she sees feminism in relation to class and race.

A white teacher stated:

Yes, I am a feminist but not at the expense of class. Feminism is part of a wider political struggle. You can't have socialism without freedom for women. Feminism is about more than being equal in this society; it is about a better society.

Discussion on class suggests alignment with the Marxist feminist tradition. Within Marxism it is considered impossible for one to obtain genuine equal opportunity in a class society where the wealth produced by the powerless mainly ends up in the hands of the powerful few. Agreeing with Engels, many Marxist feminists claim that the oppression of women has its origins in the introduction of private property and that gender inequality derives from capitalism. It is not an independent system of patriarchy. An area of agreement from women in our study was on the subject of self-identity and definition in terms of class. Many women described themselves as born and raised working class. Having become teachers, they are now labelled as middle class but they do not necessarily or comfortably self-identify as such.

Teresa De Lauretis stresses the urgent need for a move away from a single notion of feminism and the avoidance of an additive model whereby white middle class feminism is subjected to the adding of 'elements' (usually black and/or lesbian). Addition does not mean change. She writes:

> . . . the view of feminism that is prevalent in academic discourse in spite of the current emphasis on the cultural racial and political differences that inform an indefinite number of variously hyphenated or moderated feminisms (white, Black, Third world, Jewish, socialist, Marxist, liberal, cultural, structural, psychoanalytic, etc.). Adding on race and class means in effect adding on women who are not white and middle class. To add race and class is to talk about the racial and class identity of black women or poor women. Talking about racism/classism ends up being talk about something experienced by others . . . What is needed is a process of understanding that is premised on historical specificity and on the simultaneous if often contradictory presence of those differences . . . a process that seeks to account for their ideological inscriptions.
>
> (De Lauretis, 1990, p. 116)

As Bell Hooks writes:

> In much of the literature written by white women on the 'woman question' from the nineteenth century to the present day, authors will refer to 'white men' but use the word 'woman' when they really mean 'white woman'. Concurrently, the term 'blacks' is often made synonymous with black men.
>
> (Hooks, 1981, p. 140)

Differences amongst women must be noted and discussed to move beyond an account of the condition of women that is exclusionary, avoiding a parallel with masculine accounts which exclude women. Much published feminist theory has reflected and contributed to 'white solipsism' – the tendency to think, imagine and speak as if whiteness described the world. As long as race is taken to be independent of sex, racism as independent of sexism, there is the possibility of perpetuating seriously misleading descriptions of gender and gender relations.

Spelman, too, warns against additive models, considering that these analyses of identity and of oppression can work against an understanding of the relations between gender and other elements of identity, and between sexism and other forms of oppression. She clarifies the subtlety and complexity of the issue of racism in feminism, writing that white women marginalize women of colour as much by the assumption that, as women of colour, they must be right as by the assumption that they must be wrong. The difference in recent feminisms should be understood to be a reflection of the problem of privilege. One group of women (white women) has taken its own situation to be that of women in general.

In an educational context, Minhas notes that:

> If race gender and class issues are compartmentalised, the teaching approaches and strategies developed for combating racism, sexism and class bias will be limited and less effective than they might be.
>
> (Minhas, 1986, p. 3)

Minhas advocates an integrated approach, rather than an additive one. Anthias and Yuval-Davis (1983), who described themselves as socialists working within a broadly Marxist informed analysis, point out that race, sex and class are 'enmeshed in each other' and they advocate study of this interrelationship, stressing that:

> . . . any political struggle in relation to any of the divisions considered . . . i.e. class, ethnic and gender, has to be waged in the context of the others.
>
> (Anthias and Yuval-Davis, 1983, p. 73)

Post-modern feminists (e.g. Irigaray, Kristeva, Cixous) struggle, like other feminists, to discern the links between women's oppression and oppression in general. There are broad issues for educationalists working at all levels – including the question of subsuming feminism in humanism:

> Should women passionately and pridefully preserve all that is female, or should women work to go beyond the categories 'man' and 'woman' to a pluralistic society unconstructed by gender?
>
> (Tong, 1989, p. 232)

This was echoed in our data by a woman in Higher Education

looking to '. . . a future where gender is not a relevant category
. . . It would be socialist, egalitarian.'

While gender is a social construct and therefore subject to
societal change and even conceivably elimination, the area of
biology remains problematic for feminists – it was for some
women in our study. De Beauvoir (1953), Friedan (1965) and
Firestone (1971) all describe the conditions of women's liberation
in terms of the identification of women with their bodies as the
source of oppression. Liberation lies in sundering that connec-
tion as the biological differences between men and women are
the root of women's oppression. It is women's bodies (especially
childbearing and the assumptions that society makes connected
with this) that makes this oppression possible.

Somatophobia (fear of and disdain for the body) is a force that
contributes to white solipsism in feminist thought. If feminists
ignore or accept negative views of the body, they also ignore an
important element in racist thinking. As noted by Spelman
(1988), the 'superiority' of men to women (some men to some
women) is not the only hierarchical relationship that has been
linked to the superiority of mind to body. Certain kinds of 'races'
are regarded as more body-like than others. The idea that
physical labour and caring for the physical needs of others is of
little value is part of a racist and sexist ideology. Oppressive
stereotypes involved images of lives as determined by basic
bodily functions and attributes. Women's oppression has been
linked to the meanings assigned to having a woman's body by
male oppressors; blacks' oppression has been linked to the meanings assigned to having a black body by white oppressors.

Childcare

Dinnerstein, influenced by Melanie Klein, explains the role of
childcare in the repression of women:

> So long as the first parent is a woman, then women will inevitably
> be pressed into the dual role of indispensable quasi-human sup-
> porter and deadly quasi-human enemy of the self.
>   (Dinnerstein, 1978, p. 111)

While no woman in our research articulated this, many commented on children and childcare. The majority of women in our
study were parents and their roles of double workload (waged

Figure 3.1

work and domestic work) were a factor. The effect of children on women and their careers was discussed in Chapter 2. Although we personally believe that having the finances to buy childcare and domestic support provides an option not open to many, only three women in our study commented on this:

Childcare is a major problem. The more you do the more difficult
it becomes. My job is only possible because of others.

(Inspector)

When the children are young there is the guilt and being torn by
conflicting demands. It can be done but it means being ruthless.
You have to rely on family and friends or buy childcare in.

(Librarian)

Women still have to make a choice between their career and
children. Those that are successful have other people to look after
their children (usually other women).

(Teacher)

This is not to say that women view their children negatively, but
that they are aware of the restrictions that this may place on
them in a society that does not provided adequate and/or good
childcare facilities. This is particularly important in a society
where the number of women with children in the labour force
has increased in the past years and continues to do so.

Several women recognized that the increase of men into senior
posts relates to an attempt to drive women back into the home, and
demonstrates a return to highly traditional ideas of male and
female roles. Women in all phases of education commented
on this. Many women noted the limited choices available to them,
and the convenience of teaching as a career to combine with
childcare, as we noted earlier. We commented on this in Chapter 2.

Some women mentioned their hopes and aspirations for their
children, regarding feminism as a way to counter oppression. A
part-time lecturer wrote of feminism as a way of passing on
possibilities to her children, as a source of supportive strength as
well as being another ideal to live up to, like that of the ideal wife
and mother. A librarian wrote of wanting her daughter to grow
up feeling confident in herself and her own power, and to be assertive. A teacher expressed similar views when she said 'I want to
make things better for my daughter'. Four women wrote or spoke
of their sons and their attempts and wishes for them to grow into,
as one women said 'a different, better, kind of man'. This woman
remarked, wryly, that he should, with a feminist mother and
many strong women in his life but probably would not.

Theory and practice

Many feminist educationalists attempt to integrate their feminist
theory with their daily professional practice. Classroom teachers

spoke of their feminist theory informing their management of the classroom space, children's activities, resources and interactions:

> I am really conscious that boys dominate the space and my time – and I am always trying to redress the balance – easy to say; hard to do!

> In the nursery, it is educationally really important for everyone to experience play in the home corner, on large wheeled equipment, with dolls. I have to intervene, encourage, cajole and set an example myself.

> In my school, the women's group has helped us recognize sexual and racial harassment and the implications for students' learning.

A senior inspector spoke of her decision to enter teaching as an extension of her political involvement and as a force for social change. Several other women remarked on the need to return to political activity, not staying in the realms of theory, questioning the relationship between discourse and activity, and expressing impatience with what they saw as academic feminism.

Charlotte Bunch, speaking at the fourth Feminist Bookfair at Barcelona in 1990, described the complex relationship between feminist theory, feminist/women's studies and feminist activists, regarding this to be the challenge to the 1990s (as it was to the 1970s and 1980s). She asked how we (feminists) bridge the gaps between academics and theorists, and activists. Bunch commented on the evolution of women's studies from the Women's Movement, considering that feminist theory comes from the activists, not the academics, and considering herself to be both an activist and an academic. The two are not mutually exclusive, but the area is problematic for grassroots activists (including classroom teachers) who need, but rarely have, time and space to write. Rosanna Carrillo, speaking at the same event, commented that:

> As activists live from crisis to crisis they [we] have little time to stop and think – to theorize. But we need theory that is immersed in our militancy and radicalism.

Bunch concurred that we all have ideas important to theory and that feminist academics are always engaged in strategy.

In gathering data, we too have tried to make links between the words of teachers and practitioners, and theorists and philosophers, recognizing that circumstances play a large part in determining status. The element of chance – being in the right place at the right time – was commented on by many women in terms of their career promotion and chance. The opportunities for practising teachers to participate in action research have diminished with the introduction of the Education Reform Act (1988), particularly through Local Management of Schools and the decreased role of local education authorities in the provision of inservice training for teachers (and others) in education. The hierarchical nature of the educational system does not allow classroom teachers the opportunity for self-development and influence, which might result from writing and publishing material on their practice. Bunch's suggestions (also mentioned in Bunch, 1979) for possible solutions included the use of interviews and (written up) workshops. In considering the implications for changing the world (as feminists are attempting) she suggested a framework for questioning and thinking which was influential to our own thinking and approach to this chapter:

1 How do we name – describe – reality? Our lives as women are of great diversity. There is the need to define a new understanding because our experiences are so different.
2 What is our analysis of that reality? Why have women been oppressed in different ways? Gender, Race, Class, Sexuality, Ability and Age are among the issues to consider.
3 Vision – how do we envisage? What are we working towards?
4 Strategy – how do we move? Theorists and activists must come together to build specific strategies for change.

A starting point for us in our study was the acknowledgement that practising feminists working in educational establishments are constrained by the structures of male hierarchy. The structures of establishments inhibit radical feminist practices in education. The majority of feminists in our study recognized that they needed to work within a theoretical framework of liberal feminism. Not surprisingly, many frequently used the term 'equal opportunities':

> The principal aim of this equal opportunities approach was to encourage girls and women to move into privileged and senior positions in existing educational institutions rather than to seek any fundamental changes in schooling.
>
> (Weiner, 1985, p. 8)

From Mary Wollstonecraft to today, protests are made in

education at the sexism that denies girls and women the right to participate as equals with boys and men. The recognition of the inferiority of girls' education and the need to establish equality of their opportunities is well documented by feminists, e.g. Eileen Byrne (1987) and Kate Myers (1992). Using the language of a very different political persuasion, others have noted it too:

> At all stages of the educational process girls fail to reach their potential . . . They are handicapped both in their opportunities for employment and indeed in aspects of everyday life which require a grasp of mathematical or scientific concepts . . . The education they receive is inadequate. They are entitled to expect better.
>
> (Sir Keith Joseph, 1983)

Liberal feminism focuses on redressing inequality in education and employment and on reforming sexist attitudes that sustain denial of equality. In seeking equality with men, it looks to reformation rather than radical change, remaining accepting of masculinity and male values. Liberal feminists seek equal provision and access for all. One woman in our study, reflecting the views of many, wrote, 'Of course as a teacher I want equal opportunities for all boys and girls'. This approach is 'safe' enough to have become inculcated into the National Curriculum – as one of its three stated 'dimensions' (multicultural education and special educational needs being the other two).

Liberal feminism is often criticized for its lack of analysis of social structures. Liberal feminism is seen as individualistic, tending to blame the victim and narrowing the debate to achievement and meritocracy. Equality is defined as women gaining entry into the male world with no expectations of major changes in that world. Liberal feminism regards patriarchy, with its accompanying sexism and misogyny, as a societal aberration, which can be eliminated, rather than as an an essential component of exploitation (O'Brien, 1986). A harsh view of liberal feminism is that it seeks:

> . . . a slice of the capitalist action without changing its structure. All women's rights wants, and all it will get, is a change in the genitalia of the people at the top.
>
> (Bunkle, quoted in Middleton, 1984, p. 77)

While liberalism appeared in many of the responses we received, there were women whose views were clearly radical. Again, we do not wish to 'label', recognizing the complex nature of our own relationships between professional, public and private persona, and conscious of the role and impact of feminists working for change within the educational system. Furthermore, within liberal feminism there are many attitudes:

> Some liberal feminists favor monoandrogyny – the development of a single or unitary, personality type that embodies the best of prevailing masculine and feminine gender traits.
>
> (Tong, 1989, p. 31)

and there are radical possibilities within the liberal tradition (Eisenstein, 1986):

> I do a lot of equal opportunities work but my political perspective is not liberal. As a radical feminist I think you have to try and work within the system to change it. That sounds a bit contradictory, but I'm a teacher and children are in the school system.
>
> (Primary Teacher)

Within an identified radical feminist tradition, patriarchy is seen as the fundamental form of women's oppression. With its 'the personal is political' slogan, this perspective involves the appropriation of women's sexuality and their bodies. Sexuality is regarded as a major site of male domination. Male imposition of notions of femininity on women has the intention of restriction, whether in schools (Jones and Mahony, 1989), administration (Shakeshaft, 1987) or sexual relationships (Jeffreys, 1990). Radical feminism recognizes that violence is a form of social control. This has relevance in the educational context. Although physical violence is now illegal in the British education system, age, size, sex and status of teachers make for a power imbalance. Use of all or any of these can be ways of gaining and keeping control over children and young people. Schools, as part of a wider society, reproduce patriarchal relationships.

Feminists are viewing styles of teaching, learning and managing through a different lens. This is not simply an attempt to add women and girls to the equation but to radically alter the status quo. Ways of working, as well as what is learnt, are concerns for feminist teachers, as they were for us as feminist researchers.

CHAPTER 4

Women Researching Women

. . . by methodology I mean both the overall conception of the
research project – the doing of the research – as well as the choice of
appropriate techniques for this process . . .

(Klein, 1983, p. 89)

I define research for women as research that tries to take account of
women's needs, interests and experiences, and aims at being
instrumental in improving women's lives in one way or another.

(Klein, 1983, p. 90)

A feminist methodology

Feminist methodology begins with the view that women are
oppressed and is as such politically committed to changing
the position of women. The process of researching and investigating, as well as the product, has importance.

Our project attempted to discover and uncover some of the
links between women's private and professional lives and their
attitudes to feminism. Like many others, we regard feminist
research as essentially political, concerned not only with expo-
sure but also with change. We regarded ourselves as activists,
whilst still trying to theorize and examine existing theories of
both feminism and management for practical purposes. We did
not regard ourselves as 'outside' the research but rather as part
of it, with our contributions being incorporated and our interpretations recognized.

We focused on the experience of women managers because we
believed that the female experience in education is qualitatively
different from the male experience. Because of our own experiences of being managed by women and men, and being women
managers ourselves, we were conscious of the impact of gender
on management.

Looking at how to conduct our research, we sought alternatives to established ways, and read what we could on feminist research techniques and methods.

Framing guidelines for feminist research, Mies (1983) suggests that 'spectator knowledge' be replaced with active participation in actions, movements and struggles for women's emancipation. She criticizes 'ivory-tower feminism'. We looked at the relationships between theory and practice in Chapter 3.

Scott writes on her use of feminism and qualitative methods as stemming from a desire to say:

> . . . something meaningful about women's lives and also about my own, and to attempt to fill the enormous gap in sociology on the subject of women's experience.
>
> (Scott, 1985, p. 69)

We wanted a method that would put women at the centre of the discourse, not as 'the other' in relation to men (as identified by Simone de Beauvoir in *The Second Sex* and subsequently expanded by many feminists). In the study of educational management, as elsewhere, women are usually either invisible or added on.

Invisibility

Writing on women's invisibility, Du Bois notes that:

> Feminist scholars are engaged in almost an archaeological endeavour – that of discovering and uncovering the actual facts of women's lives and experiences, facts that have been hidden, inaccessible, suppressed, distorted, misunderstood, ignored.
>
> (Du Bois, 1983, p. 109)

Added on

An example of the 'additive' model is Smyth (1989) *Critical Perspectives in Education Leadership*, which includes a chapter on feminist management by Blackmore – and no mention of gender elsewhere in the volume. This fairly common practise of isolating women in one discrete chapter, or as an afterthought, presents women as a 'deviant other' group outside the 'real' world, in this case of male administrators and managers.

Androcentric research methods

Shakeshaft (1987) points to the methodological weakness in educational research where the issue of gender is ignored. Androcentricity takes male as norm for granted and thus considers itself able to ignore gender. Challenging this, by placing women in the centre and making women and women's issues the starting point, necessarily leads to a criticism of androcentricity.

The theories and methods available through social science and the field of educational administration do not offer feminists particularly satisfactory ways of investigating ideas of women's oppression because those ways are founded on an androcentric world view. This view is evident in many sociology texts. Some of the examples are old, such as Bell and Newby (1977) *Doing Sociological Research*. This is, however, still a standard text on recommended reading lists. Its male-centredness, common in much academic research, gives a message to today's readers, just as it did to those a few decades ago. The (all male) contributors to this book have, as evidenced in text and bibliography, excluded women and gender issues and have chosen to portray the world of sociology as defined by men. Similarly, and more recently, Cohen and Manion (1989) *Research Methods in Education*, which is widely used in teacher training, makes no reference to gender issues in its text and none to feminist methodology in its bibliography. This is perhaps surprising in a new edition of a work providing much needed information on research methods in education. In its introduction, under the heading 'The Search for Truth' we read that:

> *Man* has long been concerned to come to grips with *his* environment and to understand the nature of the phenomena it presents to *his* senses.
>
> (Cohen and Manion, 1989, p. 1; italics added)

Cohen and Manion ignore the observation made by Marten Shipman (1985) that feminist research has revealed a different reality and has exposed the bias inherent in previous research. Shipman (1988) suggests that fundamental to male-centred social science were (and, we argue, remain) biological fallacies about women. An example of such biological fallacies is the nineteenth century eugenics debate (Dyhouse, 1981). Learned men of this period decided – and decreed – a two-sided argument. First, that ladies were not capable of highly intellectual activities and second that they should not undertake much intellectual activity. The reason for the first was their wombs; the risk, if they did the second, was damage to their wombs. The fragility of upper and upper-middle-class women was seen as highly desirable; to the men of those classes at least.

An objection to the practice of studying male behaviour with male methods and to the assumption that these results and methods can be applied to all human behaviour is basic to feminist methodology. Dorothy E. Smith refers to the 'peculiar eclipsing of women', arguing that men's standpoint is represented as universal and as an integral part of the development of a capitalist mode of production. In common with other feminist researchers she comments on the the male domination of thought:

> The universe of ideas, images and themes – the symbolic modes that are the general currency of thought have either been produced by men or controlled by them.
>
> (Smith, 1988, p. 198)

Critical of androcentric, male styles of methodology, Liz Stanley and Sue Wise (1983) and Renate Duelli Klein (1983) note that feminist research, too, can and does continue elements of androcentricity. We operate within a social framework constructed and controlled by a value-laden system that has assumed neutrality. Feminists, along with everyone else, are a part of this system and influenced by it on all levels of consciousness. Stanley and Wise explore the pervasiveness of the male paradigm, commenting that:

> We become a part of the research community by enacting the same rituals the others have done before us . . . Frequently we fail to report or discuss the contradictions between experience, consciousness and theory, because the paradigm we work with tells us that these are unimportant or non-existent.
>
> (Stanley and Wise, 1983, p. 154.)

In attempts to avoid and challenge androcentricity, feminists are trying to develop new methodologies within new paradigms. Two of Kuhn's (1962) many uses of the word paradigm are 'a new way of seeing' and 'something which defines a broad sweep of reality' (quoted in Klein, 1983, p. 98). Klein observes that these could approach a definition of feminist scholarship 'because they affirm one of the principles of feminism to remain flexible and open for change' (Klein, 1983, p. 98). Helen Regan quotes Frances Maher and Mary Kay Tetrault on feminist methodology:

> A conceptualisation of knowledge as a comparison of multiple perspectives leading towards a complex and evolving view of reality. Each contributor reflects the perspective to the person giving it, each has something to offer. This methodology replaces the search for a single, objective, rationally derived 'right answer' that stands outside the historical source or producer of that answer. Instead, it aims for the construction of knowledge from multiple perspectives through cooperative problem solving.
>
> (Regan, 1990, p. 565)

A major criticism of scientific or positivist methods of research is that the researcher often remains invisible in the research process. Stanley and Wise (1983) outline the positivist model in three stages:

1 Consideration of theory, identification of general problems within a field of enquiry, leading to the formulation of a hypothesis.
2 Collection of information using a series of technical devices.
3 Analysis and interpretation of data.

In social science there has been a move away from deductivist research towards more 'natural' and inductivist methods. There are many variations of the latter methods, which can all be classified as 'bottom-up' or qualitative perspectives. In social phenomenology and symbolic interaction the research is primarily concerned with the interpretation of social action and meaning. Yet much of what is described as naturalism is a recasting of an inductivist version of positivism. Instead of theory preceding research, the research provides the basis for the development of theory. Research reports tend to utilize abstractions rather than give the reader an account of what happened; the report being based on a logical development of an argument, not on the temporal occurrence of events. These methods do not allow feminists to engage in research as a political activity because they are governed by the rules of the social science academic work, a male hegemony. Stanley and Wise provide a critical summing up:

Feminist reliance on naturalism and 'soft science' is insufficient. It
stems from insufficient feminist criticism of positivism, insufficient attempts by feminists to find better alternatives.

(Stanley and Wise, 1983, p. 160)

A feminist research process may include emotion and involvement as a central factor in locating and describing women's
experiences. Scott points out that it is misleading, however, to
assume that feminist research and qualitative research (or, more
precisely, in-depth interviews with women respondents) are
synonymous, although:

What seems significant . . . is the way in which a desire to do
valid feminist research has caused researchers to cut across
the usual methodological boundaries between qualitative and
quantitative methods.

(Scott, 1985, p. 71)

Feminist methods versus non-sexist methods

Feminists from a range of theoretical perspectives have struggled
to find alternatives to the androcentric method of social science,
using more intuitive and phenomenological approaches.

Stanley and Wise argue for a radical rethink about what
constitutes research, including rejection of 'this imposed language' and a need to construct 'our own social science, a social
science which starts from women's experience of women's reality'
(Stanley and Wise, 1983, p. 165). The research process is
grounded in the personal politics of the researchers and recognizes the confusions and mistakes that happen. Debunking a
myth of impersonal research, they write:

. . . and so we believe that all research is 'grounded' in consciousness, because it isn't possible to do research (or life) in such a way
that we can separate ourselves from experiencing what we
experience as people (and researchers) involved in a situation.

(Stanley and Wise, 1983, p. 161)

Their comments on the emotional involvement of the researcher,
on continual theorizing and attempts to explain situations were
pertinent to the experience we had in conducting our research
and influential in our analysis of our project.

'Grounded theory' contrasts with views held by Eichler,
who presents a technical solution to the problems of sexism in

research. She states that 'the trick is to develop criteria that help us determine which solution is appropriate when.' (Eichler, 1988, p. 14). To do this, Eichler constructed a non-sexist research checklist, and she directs the reader to a text reference that will provide a solution to the problem. For example, if the problem is one of language that over-generalizes the experiences of women, advice is given on the use of non-sexist terminology. Eichler's approach is based on reforming and improving the methods of androcentric research. She presents sexism as a problem that can be solved by correction, as opposed to fundamental and revolutionary change in the *status quo* of academic tradition.

The research and working together

We questioned the relationship between feminism, power and women in management positions in education in our research project, trying to uncover some aspects of individual women's experience in education. As we have stated before, our sample was not representative in any way, nor did we try to generalize about women's experience from the data we obtained. Rather, we resisted accepting either of these ideas as meaningful. The research project itself and qualitative methods we used reflected our subjective approach.

In one of our first meetings we established a set of principles for ourselves, based and derived from our individual feminist theoretical viewpoints and books and articles we each read. We agreed on the following:

- We should avoid the subject/object divide found in traditional researcher/researched relationships. We should not exploit the women concerned.
- The tapes and questionnaires should be absolutely confidential to the four of us to protect the women in their employment positions and to encourage frank discussions.
- The women interviewed should be given opportunities to question us and to direct the interview. The interview to be set-up to be flexible enough to allow for dialogue as well as responses to questions – we too should be prepared to disclose information about ourselves.

- The experience of the interviews should be taken into account and include the time and place of the interview and level of rapport between the two women – interviewer and interviewee.

How we worked as a group of four, as well as what we did and why we did it, was a major factor in our Open University dissertation, important to the choice of the subject we researched and the techniques we used.

Influenced by feminist researchers and wanting to place ourselves in the process, we considered working together to be intrinsic to our research methodology for the dissertation. We briefly describe the history and the process of our experiences of working together. We were encouraged to record our process by many of the women in our study, who expressed their interest in this fairly unusual collective venture.

Initially, we decided to use a taped interview to collect data. We drew up an interview schedule with open-ended questions. We regarded the interview as fairly informal and flexible with both interviewer and interviewee able to alter the sequence of questions. At a later stage, we included written responses from women we were unable to interview personally.

After each interview, the tape was transcribed selectively. Notes were written on the location, time and personal responses to the interview, together with any other comments the interviewer felt would be relevant for each of us to share. As well as exchanging written information, we spent a lot of time discussing the interviews and information we collected. We discussed the similarities and differences that emerged from this data. It was through this discussion that we realized that we could not, and in fact did not want, to categorize women.

Profile sheets provided us with personal details of the women – age, position in family, post, salary – and gave them the opportunity to self-describe. We separated these from the rest of the woman's contribution, using a simple numerical code to cross-reference.

The product of our collective work is not the same as the result of a simple combination of four individual contributions on an agreed subject. In the writing of early drafts, there are sections that were written by two of us, and in some cases by all four. In sections drafted by one of us, others contributed initially with notes from our reading of the literature, and later in redrafting and editing.

History

The four of us were part of the 1988 Inner London Education Authority block-booked group, studying the Open University 'Gender and Education' MA module. Helped by regular meetings, a strong and supportive group developed. Towards the end of the 1988 module, the idea was mooted that we work together in the final module on a joint dissertation. This was discussed again, and in more detail, during 1989.

Most students of the original group continued with the degree, moving on to study a range of modules. Networking continued both within and across these modular groups. Many of the women from the original (1988) group stayed in regular contact. This was partly through the meetings held to discuss the publication of our (edited) essays *Reluctant Masters*. There were social and supportive elements to our meetings at this time and many of the friendships that had begun in 1988 continued.

When the *Reluctant Masters* was published late in 1989, a group of us continued to meet to discuss plans for the following year's module. At first, ten women were interested in working on a joint dissertation, which we discussed with Gaby Weiner, our tutor. Early meetings (September and October 1989) were held to consider the feasibility of the project, possible areas of investigation and the implications of working together. Eventually, four of us decided to work together and were given permission by the Open University to do so.

We were all clear that working together was anything but a soft option, and that it would require a high level of commitment to ensure sharing responsibility and all aspects of the work-load.

All too often research reads as if it were a seamless activity. Many women asked us questions about our research – what were the problems? How long did it take? How did you do it as a group? How did you fit it in with the rest of your lives? In answer to some of these questions and to further demystify the research process we have included a brief chronology of the original research and this book.

December 1989
We searched British and American databases for relevant literature. We discussed interviewees and collectively drew up a list of women, to whom we then wrote. We placed advertisements in *The Voice, Spare Rib, ILEA News, The Guardian, Sesame* and *Research Intelligence*. As replies were received, we shared the task of contacting and then interviewing women.

January 1990
We had the first of our regular meetings. We arranged a programme of evening and weekend meetings for the next six months. An early task was the devising of the interview schedule/questionnaire (later referred to as interview guidelines) on which we worked collaboratively and which we trialled on one of us. At subsequent meetings and in consultation with our tutor the schedule was refined and amended. We started a diary, recording discussions held and decisions made at each meeting. We shared out tasks – and discussed problems as they arose, for example, we had to use one return address, with the result that one member of the group received all correspondence, creating an imbalanced workload. We discussed a timetable for the collection of data, and for literature reviews.

March 1990
This month, when we met at ILEA County Hall, was difficult. Two of us were unsure of employment after 31st March 1990 and very tense and often preoccupied. During March, in particular, ILEA's abolition was always on, at least, our hidden agenda. We all acknowledge it as a traumatic experience affecting us, and affecting many of the women we interviewed, deeply.

March and April 1990
Most of the interviews took place. Subsequently, they were transcribed individually and discussed collectively.

March–June 1990
Writing and reading: We read most of the books and articles cited in the bibliography, and others we found through our literature searches, and shared the notes we made. We wrote, individually, on feminism, on the abolition of the ILEA, on

power and on management. We did this writing partly to inform each other and partly to develop our writing skills.

During this period our work progressed rapidly and the bonds between us strengthened. However, we failed to recognize that this intensity would create problems for others. With hindsight we recognize we should have negotiated ground rules and mutual expectations, especially with our tutor, at the outset of the project.

July 1990

We co-ordinated our holidays, and spent a week at the end of July together. This was a period of intense learning as well as productivity and it provided us with the continuity we had all found lacking in the year. During this week we reflected on our working together and the advantages and disadvantages of this method.

We immersed ourselves in the data! We shared insights, memories from interviews and made links we would have found difficult to make as individuals. We had to work out ways of interrogating the data and did this by examining relationships between feminism and power in both written responses and tape transcripts, discussing each woman's contribution individually and identifying trends and common areas.

This week was a valuable learning process for all of us. We constructed our timetable for the remaining two months, recognizing that there would be major changes in the working lives of some of us from September and that August was the holiday period for three of us. We could not meet as a foursome in August but we arranged times when two or three of us could be together. We finalized decisions on structures and, to some extent, on text. All the major sections were drafted, although in varying stages of completion.

August 1990

As predicted, this was a difficult time as we rarely met as a foursome. The deadline, together with other commitments (both personal and professional) put us all under pressure.

September 1990

It was no longer possible to share tasks equally as in the earlier phases. Two of us, working in Higher Education, made time to work together in the evenings in the critical final stages. For the two working in the schools sector, the start of the school year took priority during the week. Yet we met and worked together every weekend in September.

Writing the book – 1991

From the beginning of 1991 we met together and submitted a proposal for the book to Open University Press. We started to rewrite parts of the dissertation because we were now writing for a different audience. Since finishing the dissertation there has been an increase in interest in women and management and we found more publications on the subject. Quite early in the year Anne decided that she did not have the time available to write the book. From September onwards the three of us worked nearly every Saturday. We had learned a lot from our previous experiences. We worked together at the weekend rather than in the evenings as we had found before that evening meetings were very tiring and usually unproductive. Getting and signing the contract in October 1991 gave us the impetus we needed to submit a draft of the book by the end of January 1992.

Aspects of working together

It was challenging and creative! We debated and questioned the work continually. We needed to reconsider form and content. We were stimulated to think further and deeper.

The experience of sharing responsibility, in our view, can be both liberating and demanding. Liberating in that we have the scope to discuss freely, share thoughts, doubts and anxieties as well as the tasks; demanding in the need to retain firm commitment to meetings, deadlines, the interview schedule, the principles of collective work, etc.

We shared the weight of responsibility about confidentiality of interviews. Interviewees had often been open and vulnerable – initially, we had not anticipated this level of emotion and had under-estimated both the sensitive areas touched on by our subject matter and the stress caused to ourselves and many of the women we have interviewed by the abolition of the ILEA. We have been able to talk together with trust in each other's discretion, and have been able to give each other the support needed. We were supportive of each other in dealing with the doubts about the viability of the joint dissertation. We all believe that working together is a positive learning experience and can be effective for a research project. Significantly, the women we interviewed expressed interest in the project not just because of its subject but also because of our way of working. Many shared our excitement.

We were able to interview a much larger number of women and thus collect more data. We shared our readings – covering a wider range than individually possible. We enjoyed and found stimulating our differences in perspective and experience and we think this enriched the dissertation.

We recognized the responsibilities involved in a highly structured joint venture. We do not all have the same skills or knowledge but we are able to consider and use this diversity positively and not exploitatively.

Time – or rather lack of it – was our major problem. Writing and discussing as a group took a lot of time, as it is slower than working alone. Meeting after a day's work and on Saturdays added to stress. In addition the time-consuming process of interviewing was usually done in the evenings. An issue we discussed was the 'displacement' of partners, lovers, friends and family. We recognized that we became an in-group and others would feel excluded.

Stress – and in some cases illness – was a factor. But we felt that one of the benefits of this project has been its stability through our lives, with the supportive relationship established between us. It has been a strong thread through a rough time. The work, the way of working and the common experience we shared was a strong focus in our lives. This created another problem, as it had consequences for our relationships with other people. We all prioritized the dissertation over our social lives. The commitment to the work and to the group was more than a time commitment – it was an ongoing intellectual stimulus and demand.

We supported, encouraged and reassured each other. We made our weekend sessions of working together easier and more pleasurable by preparing and eating good food. The level of panic was not high, partly because of our support to one another and partly because we were aware of the difficulties from the outset and had planned regular meetings. We adhered to the contracts we made at the beginning of both the dissertation and

Figure 4.1

the book. There were periods of lull for each of us, but not simultaneously. We also found individual ways of coping with the stress. Two of us took up (and then gave up) sporting activities – a way to distance from the intellectual activity and provide relaxation. Two of us (almost three) became involved in therapy. Three of us abandoned housework – the fourth used it as a displacement activity until the last month.

Technology

We would not have been able to complete the writing up and organizing of the dissertation or this book without word processors. Our word processing skills developed exponentially but disk damage and unknown factors caused hysteria!

Without the use of tape recorders we would not have been able to collect the extent of data from interviews; again there were problems. For example, several tapes were of such poor quality that the data was barely usable.

Our research method

Interviewing

Roberts (1981) and Oakley (1981) use their own experience of interviewing women to question the validity of 'hygienic' research rules of objectivity and non-involvement. Both note that methodological textbooks emphasize the interview as a mechanical instrument of data collection, which functions as a specialized form of conversation. In this process, the interviewer needs to elicit information from the respondent in a detached, 'professional' manner so as to remove the risk of data contamination. Stanley and Wise (1983) argue that the principles of detachment, 'truth' and non-involvement remain at the centre of 'naturalistic' methods. In this view of social science, there are two recognized states of being – the researcher and the person. The latter is required to stay out of the research process, for to admit involvement is to admit failure. Roberts (1981) considers, too, a more sophisticated style in which the interviewer acts as psychotherapist, using non-directive techniques to encourage responses. Both Roberts (1981) and Oakley (1981) report that their experience of interviewing differs from this 'naturalistic' method, with a relationship existing between interviewer and interviewee. We too regard the interaction as part of the research process. We recognized this in our interviews. Despite the schedule there was an unpredictable element; no two interviews were the same because each relationship and interaction was unique.

Our interviews

There was some skills training between the four of us, in particular trialling the interview and constructing and refining the questionnaire, which we renamed 'interview guidelines' in the course of the work. As a group, we benefited from the opportunity to prepare together for the interview experience. Our reading on interviews as a method in feminist research (particularly Oakley, 1981; Roberts, 1981; Stanley and Wise, 1983; Nielsen, 1990; Stanley, 1990) influenced and informed our thinking and affected our practice.

We recognize that our research is subjective and located within a place and time. Each interview shows a 'snapshot' of a woman at a particular time. We believe that we would be different interviewers now; next year, and that even the time of day is a contributory issue in research. We recognize that time and place have an effect on both interviewer and interviewee. The effect of the abolition of the ILEA was noted, too, by several women we met subsequent to the interviews, partly as an explanation for the emotionalism that they recognized was linked to personal insecurity and the anger and disillusionment felt at the end of an era.

We are aware of the influence and limitation that being white women has had on our research, especially in face-to-face interviewing, and on our interpretation of data. The ongoing debate on the relationship between interviewer and interviewee, and multiple factors affecting this, including race and ethnicity, gender, sexuality and age, is one we appreciate.

Devising the interview schedule

We made a decision early in the work to conduct face-to-face taped interviews. Discussions between the four of us and in consultation with our tutor produced an interview schedule that we also used later as a postal questionnaire. The interview guidelines were designed to provide a framework for discussion.

We agreed that the women interviewed should see a copy of the guidelines and be under no obligation to respond. We also prepared a simple profile sheet to collect factual information about the women for statistical analysis and to help us contextualize each interview. Again, women were assured that their responses were both optional and confidential.

We had wanted to pilot the schedule before using it with a large number of women but we had no time for this. Instead, we experimented on ourselves, making small amendments as problems of understanding arose during the trial interviews, and the earliest interviews.

We contacted women through advertisements in newspapers and magazines and through our own contacts in education. Many of the women were colleagues and some were friends. We used the Institute of Education, University of London as a return address for all correspondence. We sent a standard letter explaining our project and requesting an interview. In response to the advertisements, some women sent long letters, ranging from two to eleven pages.

Our data came from three sources: interviews, postal questionnaires and letters. We interviewed a total of 44 women and received a total of 41 written responses. A detailed account of response rates and a statistical profile is appended.

The interviews

We each interviewed eleven women. Each interview lasted about an hour, although this was occasionally longer and in one instance three hours. Seventeen interviews took place at the woman's home and 27 at our or her place of work .The choice of venue lay with the woman to be interviewed. Several women expressed a strong wish to interviewed at the Institute of Education, University of London (then the workplace of two of us). Perhaps this is related to a perception of the status of that institution.

We tried to make the women feel at ease in the interviews and to arrange times and places convenient to them, taking dual roles into account. Before the interview started we stressed that not all questions had to be answered and that we could be asked questions too. Confidentiality – an area of concern for some women – was assured.

An example of an interview

(This is a composite)
We wrote to Alice, a Head of Department in an outer London secondary school, asking her if she would be interviewed. She wrote back agreeing. Sue telephoned Alice to arrange a meeting time and place. Alice asked for the meeting to take place at her school at five o'clock. Sue briefly outlined the scope of the interview.

The interview

Alice made coffee and the two women sat in armchairs in a small, crowded office. Sue described the project, its rationale and scope and structure. She assured Alice of confidentiality and asked permission to use a tape recorder. She asked Alice if she would like to read through the schedule and keep it with her during the interview. Alice chose to do this. Sue assured Alice that she need not answer all the questions. Alice was given a copy of the profile sheet and asked if she would like to fill it in at the end of the interview. Sue asked Alice if she wanted any further information or clarification. The interview followed the sequence in the schedule. There were two short interruptions.

At the end, with the tape off, Sue asked Alice how she felt about the interview, if she would like to ask any questions, and if she would fill in the profile sheet.

Written responses

Women responded to our advertisements and listings. This presented us with a problem we had not anticipated. We were all in full-time employment, all based in London, and had no financial grants to undertake the research. Time and, to an extent, money, prevented us from interviewing women who lived and worked too far from our own homes and places of work. Some women, too, were so busy we were unable to arrange times to meet them.

We recognized the commitment of the women who wished to participate, and the arbitrary nature of our locality. We felt obliged to acknowledge the contributions of the women we were unable to interview, and therefore sent them copies of the interview guidelines, identical in content to that used as a basis for the interview but with a more appropriate layout, asking if they were prepared to respond. Individual letters were sent with each questionnaire. In addition, some women wrote lengthy and very personal responses to the advertisements. We wrote back to these women, often enclosing a questionnaire. We have included some of their original contributions.

In analysing data given in a written form, it was interesting to note the variation in the length of reply to questions, and we were able to detect reflection/hesitation in the form of changes of pen, deletions and additions. A few women wrote covering letters expressing their feelings on the process and subject, and noted the cathartic nature of responding. As with the interviews, many women expressed real curiosity and interest in our research, and wanted to be informed of our progress and results. We hope this book meets the need.

On being feminist researchers – our experience

We wanted to unite subject and object, escaping the traditional interview relationship. However, we have to acknowledge our naïveté and inexperience. Conducting the interviews was an important part of the learning process for us, none of whom had had much previous experience of interviewing. On reflection, we think we were wrong to conduct so many interviews so quickly (March–April 1990) especially as this was a period of unusual turmoil viz. the breakup of the ILEA. In addition, these interviews were conducted before we had all read and discussed key texts on research methods. We attempted too many interviews for the time allocated to the dissertation and collected an unmanageable quantity of data. We seriously under-estimated the time needed to arrange, conduct, transcribe, share and discuss the interviews.

We faced a dilemma and conflict between pragmatism and ideology, having to be pragmatic although this forced us to compromise. For example, we know we were sometimes superficial and arbitrary in our analysis of the information given so generously by women. Also, although we were all initially elated by the interviews, the pleasure diminished as time pressure increased and the task of interviewing and transcribing became stressful and sometimes a chore. Although we had discussed and agreed on self-disclosure, we faced a dilemma when interviewing women who stated views we did not agree with. Independently, we decided not to intervene and thus we may have appeared to accept views that we would, in another situation, have challenged.

In addition, women had their own perceptions of the relationship and, to an extent, their own agendas. For some, there was an element of a therapy session, which left us both uneasy about the data we collected and, more significantly, uneasy about our role and responsibility. Many women apologized for not being perfect, for not being good enough feminists and for not doing it [the interview] well enough! Lack of confidence, together with the desire for perfection was a factor for some women as well as for us. Despite our intentions as researchers, the interviews were not conversations with equal exchange. They were giving; we were getting, although it was not always that simple.

CHAPTER 5

Five Women

As we have noted throughout, women's experiences are frequently missing from the literature on management, power and methodology, or are represented in a stereotypical way. This book is one attempt to redress the balance.

All the women in our study talked and wrote about their professional and personal lives, frequently reflecting on their experiences and theoretical perspectives on education, management, feminism and in some instances power. In other chapters in this book, women's views are selected from the data we collected to make or illustrate theoretical points. This has, of course, resulted in fragmenting the individual contributions.

To give (some) women a 'voice' and to show something of the picture that we were given, we have presented five women's views in a more detailed way without the intervention of our interpretation or analysis. In selecting these particular women we avoided those who seemed very easily identifiable – we are concerned to ensure the confidentiality we had promised. We excluded those letters and questionnaires that provided a small amount of information. From the group remaining, our choice was random. Pseudonyms have been used.

We asked the five women for permission to use their contributions in December 1991. Their amendments and postscripts have been included. The postscripts make a telling point about the state of education in the early 1990s. Three of the women mentioned redundancy, one has already been made redundant.

Sarah

Sarah was a deputy head of a large comprehensive. She earned between £21 000 and £25 000, was aged between 36 and 40, and is the fourth child in her family. On our profile sheet she described herself as 'Afro-Caribbean – working class'.

Education and career

Sarah went to a London comprehensive and left with thirteen O levels and three A levels. After training as a teacher she worked in London. She became a teacher for political reasons and is still conscious of her role as black teacher. She became a deputy head after two periods of teaching and advisory work over 15 years. Although she described herself as 'not ambitious' she has not allowed herself to drift.

Obstacles

Throughout her career she has been aware of the reactions of white people to her as a black teacher, and now as a manager. In the past she has experienced overt sexism and racism, although now this takes more subtle and covert forms. For example, white teachers often express surprise at her level of intelligence and competence.

Mentors

Throughout her career Sarah has had guidance and support from influential people. She used her black women's support group outside school.

Home life

Sarah said that she got a lot of support from her white husband but that he did not always understand racism. She has one child. At times she thinks she is not a good mother and regrets missing so much of her daughter's development. She was very aware of her dual role as a deputy-head and a mother and conscious that her male colleagues do not have this problem. Her working pattern and hours of work were gruelling – she worked all hours

and was aware that she left nothing for herself. In her first year
as a deputy, she installed systems and practice to improve
management in the school and improve teachers' working conditions. She stated that her 'current madness' (overwork) had a
method behind it. When the structures are in place, she does not
intend to continue these long hours indefinitely.

Feminism, power and management

Without hesitation, Sarah described herself as a feminist. To her
this meant a fundamental belief that women should be supported
and given access to all career paths. 'Access on its own is not
enough' she said, 'It is not enough to just open doors without
positive action and support.' As a senior manager she was conscious of her responsibility towards staff and pupils.

In the past Sarah has been worried about feminism in education as she, as black woman, has felt isolated. She was concerned
about the racist nature of some gender work. She has been
greatly influenced by the work of Margaret Prescott-Roberts and
other black American feminists, who address the interplay between colonialism and the oppression of black women. She said,
'I am still dismayed by the way in which much feminism ignores
racism or fails to engage in the experience and history of black
women.'

Sarah does not feel that she has any real power other than
through good, careful management. As a black, female deputy
she consciously manages staff and pupils in a way that presents
a strong and empowering role-model. In general, she said, she
forms better working relationships with women than men and is
aware of the support and influence she provides for girl students.
She was very clear that women have a more human method of
managing people and resources which few male managers can
copy. While looking for a post as a deputy head she deliberately
chose schools with female heads. She said 'The head of my current school is a feminist and good to work for. She has a clear
view on equal opportunities.'

Despite Sarah's hopes to empower staff at her school she commented on being very constrained by the Education Reform Act
and the poor consultation procedures of the new education
authority for whom she worked. She was disappointed that pro-
mises made by the new authority have not become a reality and

there appears to her to be little progressive thinking in terms of equal opportunities and educational practice.

Dress codes

Sarah said, 'I wear the power-dressing uniform and know precisely what I'm doing! I am acutely aware of the games people play, and don't hesitate to play them to my own advantage.' She said that both she and the head at her school enjoyed the game of dressing up to get instant respect and authority. At home they both dressed completely differently.

The future

Sarah was absolutely sure that she did not want to be a headteacher as there was nothing to attract her to 'such an awful post'. She had no particular ambitions other than to write and enjoy her home life.

Janet

Education and career

Janet was an acting head of a teachers' centre, earning between £21 000 and £25 000. She talked of her working-class background but described herself now as white, middle-class. She was the third-born of four daughters and was aged between 36 and 40.

The interview took place in Janet's office during the working day.

Janet's experience in the B stream in primary school has given her strong views on streaming. She failed both the 11 plus and 13 plus but thinks herself lucky that she went to a secondary modern where the head had a vision about children and success. After doing well at O levels she was transferred to a grammar school where she did two A levels, before entering teacher training.

She was offered a job by her teaching practice school where she was described as an outstanding student. After two years she was offered a post of responsibility in another school, where she stayed three years. With only five years experience in teaching, she was offered a primary advisory teacher post. She did this for two years, followed by six years in a deputy headship, including a period of acting headship.

Janet described herself as a very ambitious person but she did not find headship an appealing prospect. She was appraised for headship and advised by an inspector to apply for posts but after 'taking a battering' as a union representative following the long period of industrial action in the 1980s she had doubts. She remarked, 'The extra money would have hardly kept me in paracetamol.' She spent a year as deputy head in a teachers' centre, then had a year's maternity leave. She returned to the centre where she was acting head of centre.

For Janet, going into education was a conscious choice. She had always wanted to teach. She was not aware of any obstacles earlier on in her career and was successful in every job application. However she went on to say:

> I think I'm hitting obstacles now, obstacles I suspect many, many women face who are ambitious, which are that up until two years ago I was very much in control of my career and now I think I am compromising my career . . . no, not compromising, because it is a choice, but I now have a two-year-old and I feel that you have to make compromises in terms of balancing your needs to work, your ambition, your career and running a home and having a young child.

Mentors

A local LEA inspector had been instrumental in her career moves, as a friend and an academic.

Life-style and family

She described her background as solid working class from 'up North'. Her mother did cleaning jobs; her father was a docker. She is the third eldest of four daughters. Her father believed in education for girls. Although they did not have the benefit of education themselves, both her parents considered it important. All four girls went on to further or higher education.

Support

Her family, sisters and her partner have supported and encouraged her. Having children had a cataclysmic effect on her career. She had found it difficult in the early stages to do the required hours with young children. She and her partner both had to juggle their lives but she felt that there was no doubt that she had made more sacrifices.

Janet had replied to our advert because of the phrase 'women who had refused power'. She had been encouraged by an inspector to apply for a post of promotion. Although her partner was in favour, she decided that she could not apply. While she knew that she was capable of doing the job well, she felt she could not do justice to both it and her family. When the Head of Centre post was advertised she was uncertain whether to apply as she was pregnant again. Had she not had children, she would have definitely applied for promotion, but these circumstances meant she 'refused power'. She believes that education undervalues women and fails to take account of 'our dual roles as carers *and* career-women'.

Feminism

She described herself as a feminist 'though not in the radical sense.' To her feminism meant recognizing that women have different needs and that women should be proactive in ensuring that needs are met. The centre has a strong equal opportunities policy and her colleagues appreciate her feminist stance.

Power

Janet was unhappy with using the word 'power' and preferred to redefine it. She does not mind having power over others, believing that there is a conflict only when other people's rights are impinged upon. She would like to use her managerial power to enable others. She feels that many people have power over her. Her expectations of her job are in terms of service rather than power and she is disappointed because she feels that she could be doing more, e.g. INSET for staff, personal and institutional development.

Power in other areas

Janet believes that everyone has some form of power – some acceptable; some less so. She felt the area of power in the home needed far more investigation, and described her own situation, saying:

> My partner went to university, got a degree, runs his own business, would probably describe himself as a feminist in so much that he is aware of women's issues, when you come down to the rub of who does what, what the division of labour is, the balance is still overwhelmingly that I do most of the domestic work.

Women as managers

Janet had been involved in running a 'Women as Managers' course for headteachers and was acutely aware of the problems women managers face. This course had considered assertiveness, career planning and childcare, and a support group developed from it. Members shared experiences both inside and outside teaching and looked at women's and men's leadership styles. She spoke of the difficulty of avoiding the male management style, believing it important to avoid an inflexible style that does not get the best from people. She has, she said, empirical evidence that men and women manage in different ways.

Having children has made her aware of the demands women have on their time. Her staff might need time off to deal with domestic issues but she felt that they appreciated flexibility and worked harder as a consequence. Decisions are made at staff meetings where she tries to shift the decision-making to the group. The previous head had made decisions that did not take on board the views and needs of staff and so Janet had made a very conscious decision to have more collegiality in decision making, 'That 's not to say that I don't make decisions on my own, of course I do, but I think that I canvas more views.'

She spoke of the importance of women valuing their skills, particularly skills with people that enabled conflict-resolution and more collegiate ways of working. She also spoke of the futility of only valuing male skills, which might result in quicker but less meaningful decisions.

Janet's line manager was a woman. She had given Janet all the rhetoric about recognizing women with young children but was alarmed at Janet's refusal to attend 8.00 a.m. meetings. She also seemed to make a point of ringing Janet at home at about 7.30 p.m. just as she was busy putting her child to bed.

Janet does not set herself time limits. She used to work for as long as it took but now tries to work after her child has gone to sleep. Her cut-off point is exhaustion point.

She tries to handle conflicts and contradictions by doing a lot of talking. She feels that one of the reasons that she has a big in-tray is that she prioritizes time with her staff, not paperwork. Most of the male managers she had worked for got through their in-trays enormously quickly but for many it formed a large part of what they did.

Dress codes

She was irritated by the thought that this was something else that women, not men, had to consider. She said she wore skirts to formal meetings, and high heels occasionally, 'You have to conform, sometimes it is necessary to get into power dressing.' She also wore trousers for doing displays, etc. in the centre.

Gender issues in work relationships

Janet felt that her relationships with her colleagues were good but thought it important when working with men not to compromise principles but to 'play them at their own game'.

The future

A dilemma. Should she apply for the job that she was at present doing in an acting capacity? Should she stay as deputy head of centre? Should she have applied for the other job? She commented that the woman who had got that job also had young children and was experiencing difficulties. She summed up her feelings:

> I don't feel any sense of regret. I feel for her, for women. There are some superwomen, but at what cost? It makes it more irksome to see men go up the promotion stakes, not having to worry about these things. I feel more and more embittered as an ambitious person. I'm organized, I've got bags of energy. Men who have women who stay at home, they have got it all ways and for you

to do the same you have to make enormous sacrifices. Over the last year I have felt more and more bitter . . . Men have it all. Yet I have a very supportive partner and I enjoy my kids.

Postscript

Janet's story does not have a happy ending. She was made redundant whilst on maternity leave and is at present unemployed.

Jo

Jo was a senior inspector in one of the new London LEAs. She was aged between 46 and 50 and earned between £26 000 and £30 000. She is the middle child in her family. She described herself as an anti-racist feminist 'able-bodied but diminishing'. The interview took place in the evening at her home. The interviewer and Jo have known each other for a long time.

Education and career

Jo talked a lot about the local primary school she went to. She said that it was seen as 'rough' by the local community. Jo's memories of her primary school are of huge classes, testing, rote learning, etc. all geared to the 11 plus exam. Her emotional memories are very much about 'fear of failure'. The school was very white and the only black pupil was seen as 'exotic'. Jo won a scholarship to a middle class girls' school. She remembers feeling immense relief because her older sister had already done this. Jo said that the socio-economic differences between the scholarship girls and the private pupils was obvious. Jo's solution to this was to become a 'bookworm'. Again the school was rigid and all girls were tested in the first year for handwriting and elocution. Jo failed the elocution test and had to go for extra lessons, which meant missing swimming. In the fourth year the girls were divided into sciences and arts, including a 'fast stream'. The school assumed that everyone would go to university and the girls were only expected to do the bare minimum to get in.

Role models

The school had all women teachers, who were strong but no fun. Lesbianism was known about and named; it was part of the daily school life.

Jo followed the plan, four A levels and went off to a provincial university for English and Philosophy/Art. She wanted to do Geography but her A level result was not as good as her English result. Jo talked about not really speaking until she was thirty, this was connected to the elocution lessons and losing her own voice. Her three years at university were spent sitting back. Jo felt that she had done the degree before getting there. She then 'got God'. She taught Sunday School and loved it. Her careers interview at school had suggested that Jo was 'too quiet/retiring to be a teacher' but she thought teaching was a good idea; a way of being economically independent quickly. Her promotion within teaching was not planned. Her only decision was to come to London. Someone has always said 'here is this, how about it'. Her promotion had more to do with being in the right place at the right time and being appreciated.

Family's education

Mother
The youngest of nine children, privileged. She went to a local convent school then won a scholarship to university. Her mother approved of reading and encouraged it. She helped her daughters with their studies.

Father
Went to night school. He saw education as the salvation of the working classes.

Siblings
One older – brilliant. One younger. All went to university.

Feminism and power

Jo said that she was a feminist. For her, it is a sense of what it means to be a women in this culture/society/world. A way of looking at the world that clearly identifies patriarchy; the way it is organized and the way power is established and used. Jo said that it affected everything she did; that her feminism actively informed the choices she made about where to go, who with, what she read, where she objected/protested, where she put her money. Jo felt it was about being proud. People asked if she was a feminist in 'that' tone of voice, one that harks back to the nasty remarks about women who don't know their place. 'A term of abuse, the "bra burning" references . . .' Jo said that her perception of feminism had changed, and continued to change. Jo talked about when she changed from working in schools to joining the inspectorate:

> I had terrible difficulty saying what my new job was. The root of that was that I was uncertain about dealing with power. That doesn't mean that I wasn't dealing with power, or wasn't a powerful person before that. It suddenly came up front.

She talked about the relationship between the notion of being a feminist and being powerful in a patriarchal system, saying that it is one which needs unpacking, needs dealing with and has no neat resolution.

Jo spoke of the choices that are made, the decisions that are made and the actions that are taken, actions that will impinge on that patriarchal structure and make it 'better', 'easier' for other women to follow on. She felt there was a sense of a lot of women still to come:

> There are a lot of women who have been before us knocking things down and as we clamber through we are knocking more down for those to come. That's what feminism means to me.

Jo felt that there was a choice, and that is not to engage in the world at all. Other strongly political women have views that are different from her own which she respects, e.g. women who decide that they can only do the work they have to do as a classroom teacher. She believes that much depends on where one chooses to work, and on how far one views the struggle as being a sequence of different things towards the same end or whether we have to do it exactly the same:

> So whatever corruption I may accumulate as I go along in a comfortable, powerful and well-paid job, I know that's what I have got but I also know that it shouldn't blur the issues about race and class and disability, sexuality and age, etc. impinging along with

gender in the world in which I work in. It means you stay on your toes. I can see much more clearly now how ambition can work which I couldn't see when I was young. I now see that you can actually make a difference, and can respect people who stay out and do it in different ways.

Jo said she felt there was a real place for women to take positions of power as long as they use them politically, although she also felt that all power was an illusion. 'Power is given', she said:

> People wield power by the agreement of other people. You don't have to do or believe what anybody says (there are the extreme cases but we're not talking about them). We are dealing with credibility, will-power. A lot of it is in the mind and a lot of it is a collective activity even if one person ends up seeming powerful. There is no way they can be powerful without the people agreeing to that particular relationship. It's the structures that define, place limits on us – the time, the place at which we are born that inhibits us. It's nature and nurture.

Jo said that her intention was to use the power that she was given to effect change. The power she has over others is also her line managing responsibility to them. She talked about using power to effect change, but acknowledged that you could be blocked by 'bastards' in the system. The part of the system Jo found most blocking was that described as the 'democratic process'. She believes that although structures are meant to be enabling they are in fact disempowering, partly because they are cumbersome and time consuming; partly because they have all sorts of rules and regulations that are not explained. These are either intentionally or unintentionally used to disenfranchise.

Management

Jo felt the issue was one of feminist style of management rather than women as managers. She said that the stereotype of a manager is the bully; someone who doesn't care about feelings, or about how the work is done, who pulls rank – as long as the goods are delivered and he gets his own way. Jo talked about the characteristics of a feminist manager, which would be completely the opposite. This does not mean a feminist manager cannot, would not, does not take an executive decision. It does not mean that the feminist manager doesn't recognize the power relations.

'What makes a feminist manager different is her personal politics.' Jo thought that a feminist manager would perceive the situation (at work) holistically and she noted that tasks within an enterprise are differentially valued. A feminist manager should recognize the whole support network that makes her job possible. A feminist manager should treat her support workers as human beings, ensuring that their terms and conditions are looked after. If she does not do this then she is not a feminist manager.

Jo said that good discussion, debate, arguing, conflict in a positive sense were the responsibility of a manager. She believes it is the job of the manager to keep the common purpose clear, but:

> . . . how to get there is thrown into the melting pot. If someone is slacking, is being lazy (it's like being a parent!) unless you tell them you have had bad reports or what you have seen is their responsibility and therefore needs to be talked about, you have failed. But if someone makes a mistake, fucks up, that's different. If it was unintentional it's likely that you hadn't told them clearly enough, or they didn't have the right gear to do it. Then you need to unload blame, unload guilt. Tell them to go home, have a good sleep – take a break.

Jo talked about a situation where a man came into a team and thought he knew it all, and put the women down. Her answer to that was to have a row and pull rank, 'Someone like that doesn't deserve much understanding, compassion or time' she said.

Dress codes

Jo said that there was a lot of talk about bodies, earrings, colours with her work colleagues:

> It's not *Cosmopolitan* talk. It's double-edged. It's enormous fun and a piss-take but there is clearly a limit. I choose what I wear for particular occasions. When meeting with a particular group of uppity young men who try to put me down I dress up, to compose an image of authority in a conventional sense.

The jacket (out of the men's wardrobe range) is one thing she deliberately wore on those occasions:

> With women and on relaxed occasions and in fun you flaunt your body in one sense or another, even if it's only on your ear-lobes.

Jo wrote, 'The biggest difference now is that the job is neither comfortable nor secure. How about facing redundancy?'

Margaret

This was a postal response.

Margaret was a senior manager in adult education. She was aged between 41 and 45, earning between £21 000–£25 000. She is the eldest child, working-class raised, single by decision, Welsh and white.

She was keen that we kept her involved with our research and wanted to see the work when it was finished. Margaret was involved with a group of women who, like us, were doing a higher degree. The group was interested in talking with us about research methodology, feminist research, women's ways of knowing and doing.

Education and career

Margaret had a BA Hons in English Literature and a diploma in Adult Education. Her career has included theatre administration, outreach work and divisional principalships. Margaret's career in theatre work came to end because of disillusionment and redundancy. She does not have a DES teaching qualification and feels that this has been an obstacle to her being taken seriously as an applicant for posts in Further Education institutions and in some local education authorities. Margaret felt that although she planned her entry into adult education she had drifted into management. She did not feel that she has had any mentors, sponsors or patronage, though she has been influenced by Eileen Aird's practice and theory.

Lifestyle and family

Margaret's mother, father and their brothers and sisters all left school at 14. Her only brother attended a comprehensive school and then trained as a quantity surveyor. He was in a middle management position. Margaret felt that she got tremendous support from a whole range of women, both younger and older. She used co-counselling as a definite and planned activity to enhance this support. She does not have any children. She believed that many women are blocked in their careers by both childcare and patriarchy.

Feminism

She described herself as 'definitely a feminist.' Feminism for Margaret means an analysis of patriarchy, heterosexism, oppression, gender conditioning (especially of men) and an active desire to have men's oppression of women demolished. She did not feel that there were any tensions between her career pattern, position and feminism. She wrote that her colleagues, both men and women openly describe her as a feminist.

Power

Within the constraints of her budget Margaret felt that she has absolute control. She had managerial responsibility for more than 70 part-time members of staff. Margaret felt that she was structurally powerful, institutionally powerful and personally so. Her power enabled her to be active in developing access for all women. Although she felt her job lived up to her expectations in terms of power to effect change, she stressed that she was very conscious of the fact that it takes a long time.

In terms of power in other areas of her life, she described herself as 'a political activist, although at present non-party'. She was involved in networking at many levels and regarded herself as an agent of change as well as a theorist.

Management

Margaret wrote that the decisions made in her institution are made in a feminist way. Because she was at the apex in terms of decision-making, she was able to delegate and empower other women. She believed that most of her colleagues liked her style of management. She wrote, 'I try to be efficient, effective, set high standards, and I think I am approachable. My style is a woman's style because I am a woman.'

Margaret said that she did not work fixed hours but tried

not to let her professional time encroach too much. 'There is definitely a cut-off point.' In terms of conflicts and contradictions, Margaret said that she used a number of strategies, some of which were (not in order of priority but dependent on the situation): temper, negotiation, lethargy, anxiety, analysis and removal of the blocks.

Dress codes

Margaret did not feel that she followed a particular dress code. She also noted that some of the men didn't either, although the majority of her colleagues, both men and women did, she felt.

Margaret stated that she felt that her gender relations with all colleagues and students were generally good.

The future

She sometimes thinks she would like to give it all up and travel the world but basically recognizes that she is rooted in English urban social change.

Postscript

She wrote, 'Our feminist styles of research deteriorated under pressure of work into individual "competition". I have not completed my MA though I hope to do so in 1992. Here, the effects of the Poll Tax capping threats mean that £1 million is being removed from the budgets for Youth, Community and Adult Education work. A new "Community Education Service" is to be set up, with 39 or more job losses, I have received redundancy notice.

Six years of building and working for institutional change have been destroyed in less than three months. I expect to be redeployed or else cascaded out in November 1992 if there are folks "more suitable" than me at my salary banding. It's all very mechanical and equal opportunities do not enter the picture.'

Karen

At the time of the interview, Karen was in her early forties. She was head of a secondary school and earned between £26 000 and £30 000. She is the eldest daughter in a large family. She described herself as 'White, middle-class, heterosexual, advantaged'.

I had not met Karen before. The interview took place in her office. Apart from a slight problem with me and my new tape recorder, the interview went smoothly and was relaxed and enjoyable. I met Karen at a meeting some months after the interview and she commented on the stimulating effect the interview had had on her.

Education and career

Karen had no career plan and remarked that her progress was 'entirely haphazard and accidental from start to finish'. She drifted into teaching after her schooling in the private sector and university at the suggestion of a friend. She stressed that she had no ambition, but responded to personal circumstances. After eight years she took maternity leave and returned to teaching with a drop in status and salary. She remarked on this career break and its consequences, saying it is a common experience for women and virtually unknown for men, who fail to appreciate its effect.

She moved to London in the early 1980s and her career started to move upwards. She told me, though, that there were many options she might have chosen other than headship.

Mentors

She has not had a mentor but she was encouraged as a young teacher by her (male) Head of Department.

Family

Karen felt that her family was an advantage to her – a family from 'landed stock' who gave all their children a sense of their worth and encouraged them to achieve. Karen's brothers and sisters have a variety of lifestyles but share a vigour attributed to their parents and background. Karen is the single parent of a thirteen-year-old. She has thought carefully about the effect being a mother has had on her career, recognizing that her professional life would have been very different had she been childless. She said she thought she could not have taken a headship when her child was younger, and noted that it was still difficult to combine the two jobs and allocate time reasonably.

Feminism

Her response to the question was 'Yes, though I wonder what that means now.' She said that she was proud to be a feminist. She had been active in the 1970s in the Women's Movement but felt she was now 'a bit lazy in my analysis'. She dismissed the concept of post-feminism, believing this is a long way off. She said she always considered gender when examining issues. She felt that her colleagues did not regard her as a feminist. She raised the question of the moderation of her feminism, believing she has made compromises.

Power

In terms of her job as head, Karen acknowledged that she had power. She gave an example of the dismissal of a school-keeper who had been 'highly offensive', adding that while it was difficult for her to exert her power, she felt pleased that she had the power to make the decision. She described herself as a fairly powerful person who dislikes the power structures in schools. She said:

> Hierarchy, secrecy, deviousness, intrigue and all those kinds of word . . . I want to work in the opposite way, with openness, collaboration, co-operation.

Management

Karen discussed power in terms of management, detailing her attempts to create a non-hierarchical structure of working groups and power sharing. She commented on her frustration at making, as she saw it, little progress with a staff who were resistant to change, who had previously worked under a (female) conflict-oriented head and who regarded her approach as weak. She said her feminist analysis of management was crucial, and that she believed that with time there could be change, but:

The main difficulties I've had as a head have been in trying to
approach things in a collaborative way but actually coming up
against a heritage, and the assumptions of it being the other way.
I find it really painful.

Time

She laughed when I asked her about personal time and said she
did not know what I meant. She described her child as really con-
siderate. Because of her child, she had created boundaries and
time limits but finds that staff expect her to be available at all
times. She commented, too, on the extension of her role into 'the
person who washes up after meetings'.

Dress codes

She found this a fascinating area, and admitted she had considered what to wear for this interview. She said she liked to
dress with humour, never power-dressed, but was concerned to
dress appropriately. She told a story of a child challenging a
governor who was wearing dungarees. She believed that the
image of the school was important, and her clothing a factor in
the image-making.

Relationships with girls and boys

The only problem she felt she has is with some of the older boys,
'I don't know how to get through the macho' she said.

The future

Karen would like to work part-time but still be active full-time.
She would like to make a contribution that other women might
find useful. 'I'd like to enable other women to move on'.

CHAPTER 6

Power: Trick, Treat or Transformation?

Women cannot and will not be genuinely empowered until we
understand our own need for power and our deep fear of it. It is, on
the one hand, a process of demystification. We must struggle to com-
bat the effect of socialization; our induced desire for dependence and
subordination; our guilt when we deviate from the norm; our need
to accommodate and please; to avoid conflict, and to suppress our
anger and aggression. The process of demystification reveals the
effects which follow from the use of power in the 'male' culture. It is
this alienation that . . . traps both the powerful and powerless in
hegemonic structures which are cruelly dehumanising.

(Moglen, 1983, pp. 133–4)

'I was brought up to be a good little girl! And power doesn't
sit easily with that', said a teacher, making clear the perceived
contradiction between being powerful and being 'feminine'. In
addition, women are often on the receiving end of power and
have negative experiences of being subjected to it. As we already
mentioned, many women in our study said they preferred to
use words like 'influence', indicating a dislike of the associations
of power with misuse and abuse.

In focusing attention on the different aspects of power we
found the diagrammatic representation of power given by
Judi Marshall helpful (see Figure 6.1, p. 96).

Power over others

The majority of women in our study were in relatively well-paid
and senior positions in education (see Appendices) and therefore

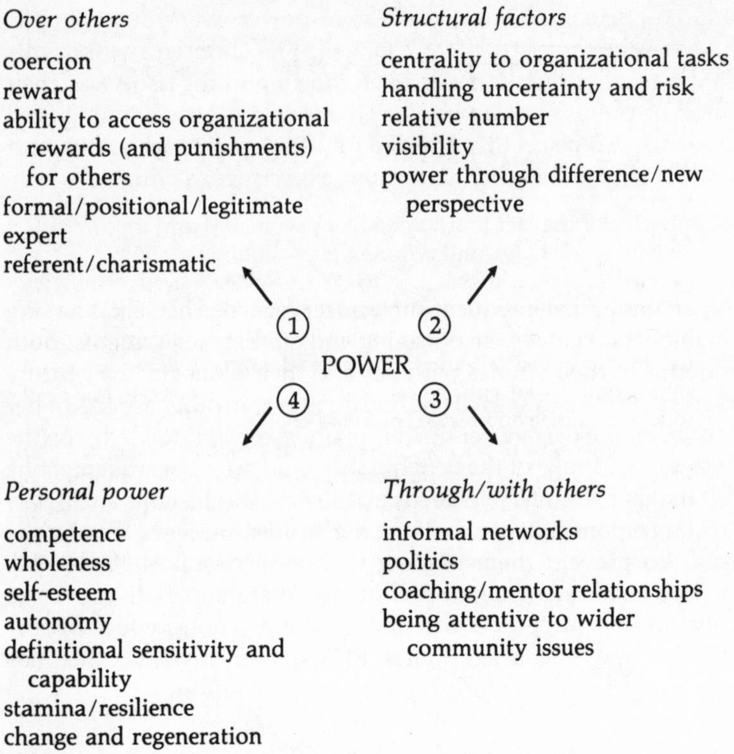

Over others   *Structural factors*

coercion   centrality to organizational tasks
reward   handling uncertainty and risk
ability to access organizational relative number
   rewards (and punishments)   visibility
   for others   power through difference/new
formal/positional/legitimate   perspective
expert
referent/charismatic

             ①   ②

          POWER

             ④   ③

Personal power   *Through/with others*

competence   informal networks
wholeness   politics
self-esteem   coaching/mentor relationships
autonomy   being attentive to wider
definitional sensitivity and   community issues
   capability
stamina/resilience
change and regeneration

Figure 6.1
Source: Marshall (1984), p. 108.

could be expected to have some power over others. We were
surprised that several women who we thought of as powerful
did not in fact feel powerful. For example, one woman said,
'I am only the head of a small college . . . and can't change much'.
People we interviewed included principals of colleges, senior
inspectors, heads, senior lecturers, professors. With few exceptions, women commented on their lack of power, although many
talked or wrote about their influence in their place of work.

Several teachers identified themselves as powerful in the
classroom, working and interacting with pupils and students.
These women were positive about the impact of their power

and no-one commented on abuse of power over young people. 'I have real power to effect change in the children I work with' said a teacher. For some women, an important issue was their view of themselves as good role-models for their pupils and students. An inspector reflected on her current high-status post and recalled her earlier classroom experience, saying:

> By virtue of the fact that I am a black woman [I am] a powerful role model for black and working class children.

A part-time Further Education lecturer regarded herself as having an important role in encouraging and guiding her students, both in terms of their studies with her and their plans for their future careers. Although she felt she had no power in other aspects of her job she enjoyed using her power, mainly seen as knowledge of 'the system' and spoke of the benefits she could offer her students. She felt that her feminist perspective gave her clear insights and a particular responsibility for helping her women students, if only, she said, 'to prevent them making the awful mistakes I made'. A deputy head said she had real power over people's lives, use of time and resources. As a feminist, she promotes equal opportunities and encourages girls to value themselves. She has encouraged women staff to apply for promotion.

Structural power

Responses covered the whole spectrum, from women who recognized that they had structural power given by the institution, to others who had no structural power. An interesting factor was the variation in perceptions about other women's power – five advisors believed they had no significant power while several classroom teachers considered that advisors were, relatively, in better positions than themselves to affect structural change.

The content of courses and the pedagogy were mentioned by a number of women as areas in which they had some power, as was the power accrued from being on examining boards and committees. For instance, one woman felt quite powerful being actively involved on college committees and academic board rather than working on the periphery. She noted that she likes to have a sense of power.

Teachers were acknowledged to have only limited power. A number of women voiced their doubts about retaining even this amount of power under the Education Reform Act (1988) and in particular the National Curriculum. The relative nature of power was recognized by many. A woman described the limitation of power in the structural context of her local education authority. She detailed the progression of power from teacher to inspector, giving herself as an example. She regarded this as a class rather than a gender issue:

> As a teacher I had very limited power . . . as head I had more power but recognized that the involvement of all staff is essential if change is to be effective. As an inspector I had power over resources, probationary teachers and in relation to heads . . . I had some power as an examiner . . . I was not less powerful than any man doing the same job. I do not believe professional women suffer oppression in the way that working class women do.

In contrast, a senior woman in higher education and a senior woman in further education said they had no structural power. They both said that they found themselves in conflict with the hierarchies in their institutions, which were antagonistic to their management styles.

A number of women told us about their involvement in trade unions, community and main-stream party politics. Some women detailed their involvement in feminist political action and black women's groups. These forms of collective action gave the women an experience of power they did not get from their jobs.

The Education Reform Act and its provision for the abolition of the Inner London Education Authority (ILEA) was mentioned as an instance of disempowerment, specifically of those working in education, generally of the children and adults of London; a painful reminder of structural power at governmental level. The ILEA was a focal point of opposition to the Conservative Government. Its stated policies on anti-racist and anti-sexist education were regarded by many as forerunners for much needed change to a more egalitarian society. These policies helped earn the ILEA a reputation for radical left-wing politics – seen by some as a reason for its abolition.

In our study, many women commented on the power of central government and the powerlessness of local government. A teacher spoke of her anger at the ILEA's demise, despite parental protest, and felt that the organized resistance was far too polite. We felt that the abolition had a profound impact on us as researchers and ILEA employees. Shortly after the end of the ILEA we wrote of our feelings. Emotions like dismay, anger, confusion, insecurity and sadness and a profound sense of powerlessness were common to us all. We recorded that:

> Doing the interviews in this state, often with others experiencing something similar, has cut through barriers and has given me a renewed sense of sisterhood. None of us feel good about its demise.

The sense of loss was a common theme – for us the researchers and many of the women in our study.

> It's like living with someone with terminal illness. It's like a death and the coming to terms with the loss; like at the end of a deep relationship. I am full of regrets, guilt and insecurity.

> Almost four weeks after the disappearance of the ILEA it's hard not to keep referring to it as if it is still there (both the physical buildings and the people). Every time I drive past County Hall I feel this sense of loss and disappointment.

There was recognition that the abolition of the ILEA was a reassertion of power by the Conservatives over an organization it could not control and an approach to education it abhorred:

> In my view the ILEA was abolished for no good educational or financial reason but to satisfy a Government whim. I fear that the chaos of London's education will increase and I ask myself what London children ever did to deserve this.

> The demise of the ILEA was just another piece of political vandalism.

Power with others – empowerment

Empowering children and students was mentioned by several women, for example, a primary head wrote about her attempts to empower children who came, as she described it, from 'economic, sexual and racial oppression'. We also heard that:

> I think knowledge is power – and part of my job is to give the children in the school access to that knowledge and teach them to find it themselves. I'm in a position to make THEM powerful!
> (Librarian)

> As a teacher of assertion training with young women I think it's important to encourage them to acknowledge and develop

their own power. In my job, I quite often see positive change in a short time as the girls start to develop their self-esteem and become really powerful young women.

(Teacher)

Practising teachers told us of work in the curriculum that tried to give students the skills to examine evidence critically. Teachers spoke of encouraging students to make informed choices and equipping them with the necessary skills so that they are better able to understand and challenge power.

Empowering other staff, especially women, was mentioned. A principal said:

One of the nice things about a job like this is that one can put into practice the support structures and help other women climb the steep side of the pyramid.

A head of a teachers' centre mentioned her power as a manager in enabling other people to have their rights. She prioritizes women, saying, 'I now put my energy into working with women.' A senior woman in higher education spoke of using her power to 'promote the general benefit of women.' A principal spoke of her role in challenging people's prejudices – she gave as an example her conflict with an interviewing panel who were reluctant to appoint a well qualified person on the grounds of the interviewee's sex and size. An advisor wrote of her work as enabling minority groups to gain access to education and to aid the empowerment of minority groups. A vice principal talked about her involvement with the issue of power and the need to deal with the moral aspects of power. Her concern is with empowering others and demystifying power, 'Women should take power, use it and come to terms with their power' she said.

Personal power

Women seemed comfortable describing themselves as assertive or as feeling powerful outside of their institutions as mentioned earlier. Most women talked or wrote about their personal power and seemed to acknowledge this more easily than professional power. An inspector articulated on power and 'self-control':

In personal life the important thing is having power over yourself – those aspects that you want to change. This comes to the fore in relationships.

Several women talked about being powerful in the context of class, money, education, physical size, race. There were women who mentioned the power they had as middle-class women with financial independence. One woman debunked the myth of the strong black matriarchal woman, noting that black women do not come from a position of strength but have come to this position out of necessity. Another teacher talked about being part of the women's movement and a lesbian in terms of the power that this gave her:

> The women's movement and the support I get from other lesbians has made me feel much more powerful as a person. Knowing there are others committed to challenging the *status quo* makes it feel easier to feel okay about your own power and how you use it.

An extract from a written response

We received a lengthy written response from a teacher. Although the statement of one individual, she expressed views common to many in our study. She provides a link between theorists and practitioners as well as a reflection of many feminists' concerns. For these reasons, we have included the contribution in full:

> How you feel about power depends on a number of influences in your life. It is usually seen as the ability to influence others' actions.
>
> *Physical power*
> The use of brute force to influence others. The use of physical power in situations of violence and incest and other forms of abuse perpetuated by men on women, whites on blacks/ indigenous peoples, etc. For me war comes into this category too.
>
> *Resource power*
> The possession or control of valued resources. These can be material or non-material; they are anything someone else wants or values. In schools it can be control of budgets, information, timetable, access to INSET, writing agendas, meetings etc. – curriculum content (now with the government/National Curriculum Council).
>
> *Positional power*
> Stems from the role conferred by an organization/institution

or is given by others. It has to be under-written by resource and physical power, or it can be based on knowledge. It confers certain rights on an individual, can involve access to information, individuals, groups, systems. This could be the source of women's power in terms of networking – maybe this is also where I have some power in that I have access to, through personal contacts, work situation and professional contacts, a whole network of women and feminists who are working in and around education.

Expertise
Skill, knowledge, etc.; the ability to get things done. This only exists if others are willing to give that skill, knowledge or status. I could accept that I have some power here too. Acknowledging that I do have or at least am seen to have some kind of 'knowledge' and maybe a 'skill'. I do, however, have the ability to get things done – I'm fairly well organized and efficient – most of the time!

Personal power
Usually includes such things as a combination of energy, competence, ability, interpersonal skills. I have some of this kind of power! However, I feel I use it in order to empower, to support and encourage others. Everyone has some skill in persuading others and therefore the ability to be powerful given that some of these skills can be learned.

At one level I *am* powerful – in that I can and do determine a lot of my life both professionally and personally. However, there are restrictions on that – restrictions that are self-imposed and also restrictions that are imposed by the structures and the society in which I live. I suppose that as a white, middle-class woman (middle class by education but not by roots) I have power in that I can and do have a relatively well-paid job (but it is insecure).

Reflecting back it's quite difficult to see where or how I have had power. I've certainly never been in awe of those who are supposedly powerful and therefore have not had to deal with feelings that go with this. I think the exception has been men and their capability to use physical power, although as a small blonde woman it has not been so much the use of that capability as the patronizing attitudes that men have to small blonde women. They are always wanting to take care of you (me). Here the struggle has been to exert myself and my own personal power – as capable and able to defend myself without needing to resort to some kind of protection.

In terms of work most of my 'managers' have been male or have been women who worked in a male way. I do not accept that they have power simply because of who they are in an organization so I do not give them power over me. My first teaching job (a part-time temporary terminal contract) although insecure was also in many ways liberating. Given that I could lose my job at any time meant that I could challenge/do what I wanted and be radical in that I had nothing to lose. The head – a man – had an open-door policy, was willing to think, was not good at being challenged but would not shut out ideas that he did not understand or necessarily agree with. His replacement, however, was a whole different ball game and we were on collision course from the word go. He was manipulative, indiscreet and totally untrustworthy – would argue that he was one of the 'new' men and 'some of my best friends are . . .' then pick people off one by one and make them insecure and therefore easier to manipulate. One of the bullies in life who cannot stand being faced with someone who tells him his methods of working are the worst possible and won't be bullied by him.

I've also had two women as line managers – both of whom were seen as 'feminists' but who worked in a male way. Competitive with each other (and others), inflexible, dictatorial and not open to change and challenge. Fortunately I was able to ignore this and, given that I had a specific brief, was able to do what I wanted, and direct my own time (a very powerful feeling especially when you have been used to being dictated to by 'pips', but also can make you work twice as hard as you need and produces lots of guilt). I have also worked with someone people thought was my line manager – but neither of us saw our relationship in that way. We worked well together in a collaborative, collective way.

In relation to the headings used, I suppose I have Resource, Positional, Expertise and Personal power. I suppose I also have some power over others, absolutely no structural power, definitely power with others and some personal power. However, it is very rare that I feel powerful in any given situation and for me the reasons for having this kind of power (if I do have it) is to share it, access it for others, spread it around, not to hold onto it in order to make myself feel powerful (power with others). Anyway, power is only possible, I think, if others give you power and you are willing to accept that which is given. As I don't see myself as powerful and believe that power is only useful for radical change and therefore only acceptable as a collective action I want others to have as much as I have. Collective, collaborative power is what will bring about change and make the world a better place. Women can and do have the potential to take that kind of power but they have to take it – it cannot be given and it's unlikely that men would be willing to give up their power anyway.

Power has all kinds of overtones of maleness attached to it which I don't like. Male power is abusive and I certainly don't want any part of a power that is like this. I do, however, like having power – personal and professional – but it's about recognizing this power, using it in a collective way and accessing it to others. However, I have this nagging sense that ultimately I am powerless and don't have any real chance to change a thing.

Ambivalence about power was an issue for many women. The points made by the contributor quoted above were echoed by many and were ones that we recognize and acknowledge – then and now – in our own lives.

Power as problematic

Imagery of power: feminism and power

Feminism has an ambivalent, often negative attitude to power – this showed in our interviews when some women expressed their dislike of the word 'power' and their reluctance to be associated with it. Power has been traditionally conceptualized from a masculine standpoint, analysing power from a position of power. Women are therefore always on the periphery, and their attitude towards power essentially one of ambivalence.

A teacher wrote to us that she disliked the word as it has connotations of oppression. Many women expressed their wish to substitute other words like 'influence'. An education consultant wrote:

I am consciously enjoying having power to get things done, but do not feel comfortable with the concept of holding power over others. I prefer people working with me rather than for me.

There was clearly dislike for power in the sense of domination/ mastery/oppression, reflecting points made by Singer (1987, p. 86):

During (the) early phase of second wave feminism, power was, for the most part, a taboo subject – something to be opposed, avoided or rejected, figured as that to which feminist theory and politics were to serve as an alternative . . . If power was essentially that from which women and other oppressed groups were absent or excluded, then women's relation to power was essentially negative.

Many women in our study appeared to be 'caught between' the male view and a feminist alternative, which we find unsurprising, as many, like ourselves, were working in environments reflecting the androcentricity of society as a whole.

Janice Raymond writes in *A Passion for Friends* that:

> On the one hand, many women tend to regard power ambivalently, as something to be avoided, something that corrupts, and something that is always used over and against others . . . many women having been the victims of patriarchal power, have assumed uncritically that power itself corrupts.
>
> (Raymond, 1986, p. 193)

In our research, power as corrupting was often mentioned. One woman said, 'Power can corrupt and suck you in.'

The examples below illustrate the complexity of power issues for women. A part-time teacher and PhD student described the ambivalence she felt:

> There are a lot of hierarchical power games in higher education which I hate. The women who get high enough to play them (I believe) have to compromise their feminism. Yet power does have a peculiar attraction and I do want some. Like most part-time teachers . . . I have no power. Students, however, tend to invest you with power and believe you have more than you do. Not all power is bad, it is just difficult to use it in good ways as things are . . . I wonder about the subtle power issues I miss because I don't really know the rules of the games.

A Media Resources Officer in a Further Education college talked about her attitude to power:

> I'm not sure that heaving yourself up the ladder to get power is where it is at because the grass roots meddling is powerful too . . . I'm surprised that I do have influence, that's because I say what I think . . . In the last year or so I have watched friends become managers . . . it will be interesting to see the way these women try to break down hierarchal structures . . . I'm interested in power and want it, but not in replicating male power.

Images and power: femininity?

> . . . we signal to the outside world through the way we stand, sit, move and dress that we are powerful, influential, assertive – and feminine.
>
> (Bryce, 1989, p. 73)

For women managers there is a range of images – a point made by a number of women who talked about a variety of styles used depending on both the context and women's self-image. Many of our findings on how women choose to present them-selves and develop their own style have been noted elsewhere. We heard from women about wearing high heels, short skirts, earrings, business suits, the 'masculine' jacket and, as one women put it laughingly, 'the listen-to-me clothes as opposed to the take-me clothes'.

Women's attitude to power relates to their femininity, how they are viewed and view themselves as women. Naomi Wolf's *The Beauty Myth* (1990) links the relationship between female liberation and female beauty. She regards the backlash against women's advancement to have been the political use of the beauty myth.

> As women released themselves from the feminine mystique of domesticity, the beauty myth took over its lost ground, expand-ing as it waned to carry on its work of social control.
>
> (Wolf, 1990, p. 11)

> The beauty myth is not about women at all. It is about men's institutions and institutional power.
>
> (Wolf, 1990, p. 13)

> As women demanded access to power, the structure used the beauty myth to undermine women's advancement.
>
> (Wolf, 1990, p. 20)

Wolf regards dressing for business success and to be feminine as mutually exclusive – women's sexuality can blot out all the other aspects. Her controversial book indicates the problematic areas of images of women, femininity and especially beauty within the women's movement.

As we noted in Chapter 1, women managers are often advised to play down their femininity. This has two functions – to prevent the distraction of men and to project a serious image:

> Serious women have a difficult time with clothing . . . because feminine clothes are not designed to project a serious demeanour.
>
> (Brownmiller, 1984, p. 101)

As Chapkis suggests in *Beauty Secrets* (1986), women have always known that how they look is often regarded as more important than what they do or how they do it. A senior inspector in our study was acutely aware of this, telling the interviewer that she makes a deliberate attempt to get people to listen to what is said rather than what is being worn. Many of the women in our study described dressing appropriately, frequently meaning dressing for an audience, within the culture of the institution and the dictates of the male gaze of the western world. Three women, all self-identified as feminists commented thus:

> I play the game – although shoes are a major problem!
>
> (Senior Inspector)
>
> I am expected to be dressed well – no jeans! Trousers are okay, but not quite normal.
>
> (Teacher)
>
> Women are under tremendous pressure to dress up. They need to be smart. Dressing for others – the man-appeal as well as the power.
>
> (Inspector)

'Appropriate' meant different things to different women. A few mentioned dressing to please/attract men, as implied by the last quotation and stated more definitely by another self-defined feminist, 'I dress to exude sexual power over men' and an adviser who described herself as a feminist – but 'defensively' – who said she likes to dress up, and feels her male manager is turned on by her mini-skirts. She told us that 'one or two heads comment on my appearance, but this is not sexist.'

Other women commented on dressing to control men, using their femininity to distract when this seemed advantageous:

> I've got a smart suit – shoulder-pads and short straight skirt. It's really useful – when things get rough at conferences I just cross my legs and flash a bit of thigh.
>
> (Lecturer in Higher Education)

For most women, power dressing implied a jacket or suit, e.g:

> I do feel the pressure [to wear] jackets, etc. I feel it often makes a difference to how you are viewed at meetings, school visits, if you look the part.
>
> (Librarian)
>
> I have to be respectable – like the chaps in suits, formal clothes.
>
> (Deputy Head)

There were other comments on power and dressing:

> I feel that to be taken seriously smart dress is essential.
>   (Ex-feminist (her description) Head of Department)

A feminist wrote that she avoided power dressing 'like the plague' but felt that other women do not as there is a competitive element. A woman who described herself as a liberated woman – not a feminist – said she feels sorry for power-dressing women, believing they lack a sense of identity and worth. A woman who said she supported feminist beliefs, though she is not a feminist herself, told the interviewer:

> In school there is an obvious divide. In my new job the competition is HOT with the inspectors in their designer suits. For women it is about power, about being in total control, chic, expensive. There are two looks – the short skirt and the high heels, and the flat heeled sophistication look – trendy. And the jewellery – big and chunky. It is difficult not to take part.

Other comments included:

> Clothes control women's behaviour. Wearing high heels makes me walk differently.
>   (Ex-head of Department)

> The Headmaster takes it upon himself to comment on the wearing of large earrings by female members of staff.
>   (Teacher)

> I dress 'smartly' and I wear makeup partly as a 'disguise' and also to look older and in part to be taken 'seriously'.
>   (Technical and Vocational Education Initiative Adviser)

Some women, for social or political reasons, will not wear 'the dress' or 'the suit'. But the clothing they chose has its own set of messages:

> I don't wear what is considered the right thing. I don't want to play that game. But there is a price and part of the reason I don't get taken seriously is the way I look. Part of it is because my shirt and trousers signal my sexuality. Don't clothes always signal sexuality?
>   (Teacher)

Feminists and connotations of power

> In my opinion it is in women's alienation from their power of being female that other female problems with power begin.
>
> (Raymond, 1986, p. 194)

Samuel Johnson wrote in 1792, in a letter to Dr Taylor, 'Nature has given women so much power that the law has very wisely given them little.' Adrienne Rich argues that male attitudes to women are a result of men's envy of women's power in bearing and rearing children – women's 'natural' power. Rich writes of women creating new life not only in the literal sense of children but also of visions and thinking 'necessary to sustain, console and alter human existence – a new relationship to the universe' (Rich, 1976, p. 262). Because attitudes are deep-rooted and continuing, social changes have not reduced sexism, misogyny and chauvinism. This remains a problem, even within the politics of the Left and Marxism. One woman in our study said:

> I am active in a liberation struggle – of men and women. But most activists believe that freedom for the people will automatically mean freedom for women. [This is] a problem for feminists because it doesn't consider the double, or triple, oppression of women. Also, power-sharing means something different to women – and it's not about just taking power. Men see that power is something to be taken and used – but I don't want that, it's too likely to become just a different group of men with superiority.
>
> (Adviser)

We found numerous writings theorizing and confirming our own views. Hartsock, introducing an analysis of an alternative tradition, comments on a qualitative difference between women's and men's understanding of power. Publishing in 1983, she noted that few women have theorized about power, and found that those who did – she cites Arendt, Carroll, Pitkin and Emmet – stressed aspects of power relating to energy, capacity and potential:

> Adoption of a feminist standpoint . . . should allow us to understand why the masculine community constructed *Eros* and as a result, power, as domination, repression, and death, and why women's accounts of power differ in specific and systematic ways from those put forward by men.
>
> (Hartsock, 1983, p. 226)

Similarly, Martinez (1988) investigates female power in the world today, comparing and contrasting this to male power, which is interpreted as the forces that have sustained patriarchy. Female power, in her view, relates to a non-hierarchical and changing world view in which both women and men will be active and creative.

Female connotations of power and powerlessness

Hartsock observes that:

> There is, after all, a dangerous irony in the fact that both feminists and anti-feminists agree that the exercise of power is a masculine activity and preoccupation, inappropriate to women or feminists, and not a subject to which attention should be directed.
>
> (Hartsock, 1983, p. 2)

Beyond this irony is the female ideal of power mentioned previously and below:

> As the human majority, and as people increasingly insisting on our own empowerment, women can utterly change the terms on which power is held or seized . . . This will require us no longer to lust after selfishness, not to be satisfied with tokenism (of the right or left), not to define ourselves as non-men or 'liberate' ourselves by imitating men . . .
>
> (Morgan, 1989, p. 327)

We stress that some women in our research who identified themselves as feminists did not feel they have had much – in some cases any – power to make effective change in their places of work but they mentioned being strong and powerful in themselves and with other women.

Using power

There is a shift in thinking, which begins when some women find their social and professional position altered. Our research looked at the shift; at women who have a relationship to power that is not wholly negative, and where they are not convincingly without power. Women we interviewed were not passive or weak and in many instances had looked closely at another way of handling the power their jobs gave them.

Janeway indicates that feminists are now 'willing to play with power'. Women need to confront power, challenging the singularity of male power and refusing to collude with it:

> . . . When the weak habitually turn their backs on power because they accept the stereotypes that undervalue them, they permit their rulers to define proper processes of governing according to the experience of the rulers alone so that it comes to seem that only one 'right way' to handle power exists.
>
> (Janeway, quoted in Singer, 1987, p. 88)

Marilyn French, too, recommends a confrontation with power. She holds the view that we need to examine power to discover its vulnerability and thus demystify (control) it. She considers power to be of a 'fragile nature, insubstantial', that it can be used positively, and that women must use it:

> . . . until all of us use our power in the public world, it will continue to be dominated by those who are driven to domination, rather than by those who wish to use power as a means to non-controlling well-being.
>
> (French, 1985, p. 544)

Singer points out that these three writers (Janeway, Hartsock and French) believe that women can examine power, take it on, yet not be corrupted by it or by their curiosity. This contrasts with Janice Raymond's views (noted earlier) and the comment from an ex-teacher in our research on power as corrupting. Singer also comments on patriarchal power as stable and relatively permanent. By French's account, we have experienced 3,000 years of the power of the fathers. She later writes on patriarchal masculinity's fear that women will become aware of the concealment and intervene; and will challenge the patriarchal position and find an alternative.

Janeway and Gilligan reject the male model of power-figures in terms of autonomy and separateness. Both favour a concept of power centred on connectedness and community. They give the example of women in consciousness-raising groups who come together to believe in their own power. Several women in our study commented on the effect of consciousness-raising on their personal and professional lives, expressing some sadness that such groups appear to be a thing of the past:

> I remember the consciousness-raising group I went to in the 70s. We really looked at the way male power controlled us – and

at how we colluded. We laughed – and cried – at how we had bought the myths of romance and male superiority.

(Advisory Teacher)

The empowerment of women, achieved by a process of demystifying power and by removing the mythology surrounding power is a subject of feminist concern, as the passage by Helene Moglen at the start of this chapter makes clear. Other feminists stress that the process is both urgently necessary and difficult:

> The ruled cannot deny their subjugation to the tyrant unless and until they are willing to deny the whole body of social mythology in which his legitimacy is embodied. Making such a denial requires both courage and intellectual force. It is possible . . . but hard and rare. The alternative is the dark alley of apathy, alienation.
>
> (Janeway, quoted in Singer, 1986, p. 97)

We believe this to be an issue in all liberation movements – and an investigation of how the mythology is enshrined in law as well as custom is an area worth pursuing in the future. It may go some way to explaining what we perceive to be Margaret Thatcher's decade of power over a relatively docile populace and electorate:

> If feminist resistance is ever to have revolutionary consequences, as women we will have to learn to exercise our powers in ways that are not only supportive and nurturing of our visions, our values, other women and ourselves. We must also be prepared to exercise our power in ways that intervene, disrupt and obstruct the workings of the patriarchal machine. If feminism is ever to dismantle male dominance, we must be prepared to use the powers we develop in ways that are critical and in some sense, destructive to the existing social order.
>
> (Singer, 1986, p. 105)

In redefining power, feminists seek to counter the emphasis on individualism, hierarchical relationships, bureaucratic rationality and abstract moral principles. In the current British and indeed world-wide political arena, with economic recession and right-wing ideologies gaining ground, we believe there is urgent need for those working in education to 'intervene, disrupt and obstruct' so as to produce a healthy climate of active learning, enquiry and development of critical and creative faculties.

CHAPTER 7

Management: A Woman's World?

Women do it different

A view from our study:

> Generally there is a difference between how women and men manage. Women on the whole respond to collaborative, responsive relationships, as a team member, and are non-competitive. Men are autocratic, hierarchical, competitive and often don't question, or if they do they don't know how to change.
>
> (Inspector)

> The strength of women managers is the support they give, both subtle and overt. They have lateral ways of thinking and working, and are capable of being supportive and supported. Working round the system. Women are very good at the detail, they have to be. Men are generally more concerned with 'the why'. Women find more ways of dealing with 'the how'.
>
> (Ex-teacher)

> I think women managers do have a different style from men. They use personal contacts much more, also formal methods, they mix the two.
>
> (Further Education Lecturer)

Shakeshaft reviewed research in the 1980s, which considered how women and men manage differently. Women in our study confirmed her summary of findings, which included observations that women:

- have a higher percentage of contacts with people;
- have shorter time on desk work during the school day;
- spend more time at home on administration and schoolwork;

- spend more time communicating (scheduled and unscheduled meetings, phone calls);
- tour buildings, visit classrooms and teachers and care for the physical environment more than men;
- are more likely to use informal styles of communication;
- develop more flexible agendas for meetings. And,
- with a woman in the chair, there is an increased chance of co-operative planning during scheduled meetings.

A woman we interviewed made the important point that acceptable styles for women and men were different in different cultures:

> The ways men and women manage are different in any one culture. What constitutes good management by women in this country equals good management by men in Japan. In this culture men are meant to be much more emotionally disengaged, rational, self-focused, individualistic in their management style, using direct assertion, physical presence, and masculinity to get their ways, an economistic tool. Women are supposed to be much better at team building, empathetic, holistic in their approach to their subordinates, but devious, laterally thinking, not so prepared to face direct conflict, going around, working on things to get what they want. Binding others to them by ties of personal fealty and affection which can be found in other paternalistic societies.
>
> (Senior Lecturer in Higher Education)

When looking at the different ways men and women conceptualize their work Shakeshaft produces evidence that women view the job more as master–teacher (sic) or educational leader in contrast to male views, which derive from a managerial-industrial perspective. Women principals pay more attention to the social, emotional and academic development of the children in their schools. They are more knowledgeable about the curriculum and value the productivity of their teachers. Anne Jones notes that female heads were much more aware of their need for training in relating to the local environment than were men. They were also more concerned than the men about training for management of change and managing inter-relationships. They placed greater value on the qualities of humour, stamina and creativity in headship than did the men, '. . . if the indication is accurate, it is a significant one for the future choice of our schools' leaders.' (Jones, 1987, p. 71).

Both Shakeshaft and Jones have identified a crucial aspect of female and male priorities in management. Our own findings mirror this, as we indicate. Other studies focused on similar attributes of the woman manager. A study conducted by Leonard (1981) found women scored high on both task and consideration dimensions. Judi Marshall's interviewees believed that women have a broader range of possible techniques for relating to others than men have, thus opening up alternative ways of communicating and getting things done. These were: listening before acting, being sympathetic, being trustworthy, not needing to dominate others, getting things done by being nice to people, making friends with people so they try not to let you down, being prepared to apologize if something goes wrong and being able to say personal and threatening things to others that would be unacceptable coming from male colleagues. These points were echoed by many of the women in our study. A headteacher remarked:

> I think we are able to be more honest and approachable. The range of possible styles is greater for us, that's one reason why I would not want to be a man. We can operate and get less flack, whereas men have a bigger problem if the softer side of their nature is allowed to show too much.

Other women in our research acknowledged differences between women and men but thought it dangerous to accentuate them, or to adopt a position that could be interpreted as being biologically determinist (as could the quotations from the head above). A lecturer in Further Education felt that it is:

> . . . too crude to say that there is a male and female style of management, we are digging a hole for ourselves. The sorts of people we are trying to influence would run a mile from anything that was described as a feminine style of management. Women are able to bring into situations qualities they have developed from their own experiences because of the range of emotional ties women tend to have which are much more varied than your average man. Not that the average man does not have the capacity to develop those things, but they have not been put in the range of situations that women have.

A headteacher stated the important point made earlier – that the different approaches are socially and culturally determined, not biologically determined.

Shakeshaft argued that sexuality and the myths surrounding it are a fundamental barrier to women in moving into administration positions as well as one of the strongest explanations for some male–female interactions. She notes that the impact of sexuality on effective leadership in organizations needs to be studied and understood. We referred to the work of Morgan, Sheppard and Ball in Chapter 1, discussing the imposed need for women to manage their sexuality and gender in ways quite different from men. The obvious (because visible) differences in women's and men's styles of dress forms part of our chapter on power, where many women considered the issues of male and female sexuality.

Shakeshaft mentions, too, the differences in morality of men and women. She cites Gilligan (1982) and Lyons (1983), who consider that men tend to follow a morality of justice as fairness. This rests on an understanding of relationships as reciprocity between separate individuals grounded in the duty and obligation of their roles. Women tend to use a morality of care that rests on an understanding of relationships as response to another. Many women in our study referred to what they considered was the more caring nature of women. Several women mentioned their own caring for women staff, and that there is a chain of responsibility, with women staff being carers too. As mentioned earlier, we heard opposing views from women in less powerful positions:

> Women are balancing all these balls in the air. I recognize this - sometimes your staff are going to need time off because they have domestic things to attend to but recognize that if you allow them that flexibility you will be paid back manyfold in other ways. And that is what men do not recognize because they don't have the ability to appreciate all those demands.
>
> (Head of Teachers' Centre)

> I give them time off if they ask for it, and send them home if they are ill or there is a crisis at home. This has a potential 'downside' in that it could be exploited. But the staff work very hard and they must know that I appreciate this.
>
> (Head)

A retired head of a primary school wrote that:

> All my staff, including ancillary staff, were seen as part of the team, they were treated as people who mattered. I gave birthday,

Christmas cards and small gifts to regular staff. I also made sure that the working environment was pleasant, with plants, flowers, art-work – and that the school was kept clean and tidy.

Building a relationship akin to friendship with her staff, and caring for the environment, were important elements in this woman's management style. She therefore echoes Shakeshaft and Schniedewind's conceptualizations of the female worlds of administration and education, with the focus on relationships with others, on teaching and learning and community building. Women, as Shakeshaft and many others note, are more likely than men to behave similarly whether in a public or private sphere, realizing that their actions reflect on all women and that the line separating the public world from the private is blurred. Shakeshaft sees the well-managed school as being identified with traditional female approaches to schooling: achievement, set instructional strategies, an orderly atmosphere, frequent evaluation of student progress, co-ordination of instructional problems and support for teachers, concluding that women possess characteristics that are conducive to good schooling. They enter teaching with clear educational goals, supported by a value system that stresses service, caring and relationships. Yet, as Shakeshaft notes, the dangers of marginality are always present for women in their daily lives. Internalizing male oppression, some women, instead of valuing their skills, down-play their power, intellect and skill in order to appear less threatening.

Women do it better . . .

Three-quarters of the participants in our study were in positions of senior management. While there was considerable reflection on and criticism of management styles, including their own, perceptions were clearly influenced by the high-status position of these individual women. We were not surprised to find that so many women expressed the view that 'women can do it better'. They are not alone in thinking this. Tom Peters, perhaps the best known of American business 'gurus', told an audience of predominantly male managers:

By the year 2,000, management as we know it, will not exist. In its place will be networks of relationships, partnerships and

alliances . . . the future will be essentially female in character . . .
A future where the characteristics and skills displayed by men
are not only worthless but may even be harmful.
(Peters, quoted in Kayofski, 1990)

A research project reported in *The Guardian* in 1992 under the
heading 'Women will take the lead in business' details a survey
undertaken in the National Health Service. The researcher,
Beverly Alimo Metcalf concluded 'That women are the natural
business leaders of the future.' Charles Handy is reported to
have ended a talk at a major conference on women and education with these two phrases:

1 Let's not turn the clock back and make women into men of
yesteryears.
2 If we treated men like women, rather than women like men,
life would be more interesting.
(Handy, quoted in Dix, 1990, pp. 10–11).

Pointing out and appreciating that 'women favour less hierarchical structures of management, they prefer to operate at work
on a set of people-centred ethics rather that totally business-
centred concerns' (Dix, 1990, p. 10), Handy would not concur
with the view of the lecturer in our study that people would
'run a mile' from a feminine management style.

We wanted to explore the links between feminine, (or to
prefer a less 'loaded' word, female) management styles and
women's roles in society and the family. We recognize the thin
and dangerous line dividing the stereotypical view of women
as selfless and caring – and therefore good with young children
in school and at home – and that valuing those qualities of
gentleness and compassion. Our research sought to find women's
professional and personal views; to give the women opportunities to tell us about the intersections of their home and work
lives. Underpinning this was our conviction, borne out by
personal experience, readings and then our study itself, that
women tend – and try – to avoid fragmenting their lives.

Management of both people and resources is familiar to many
women. It may not be called 'management' or have the status
or salary of a business manager but the role of the mother in
the home is often that of a manager. It seems that women often
bring elements from their 'traditional' domain, the home, into
the workplace. The style of managing a home and caring for

individual children may, for some women, be similar to the style of running, for example, a school with hundreds of children.

Our research and reading show that most women do not want to adopt stereotypical male behaviour. As noted before, women mentioned their concern with the ethics of management. Working for the common good, valuing common purpose, improving the learning experience of the student and providing equality of opportunity were the stated priorities of many. Many women in our study thought that women managers show greater concern for relationships and have better interpersonal skills.

Judi Marshall argues that the women managers who act from values defined as more typically female are likely to base their management style on concern for people, and work through co-operation rather than giving the task priority and promoting competition. Many of the women in our study thought of their management style as low-key or subtle and they tried to get things done by influence rather than by direct control. They were not particularly concerned about publicity or credit. They valued co-operation rather than competition.

Lambert (1989) identifies the skills women use – even if they say they are not managers:

- working with a team
- listening
- empathizing
- making decisions that influence others
- managing stress, time and conflict
- establishing priorities
- combating racism and sexism
- motivating others

But the sexism of society blocks recognition of women's abilities – and it is not just men who undervalue women. Several women in our survey stressed the importance of women not under-estimating their own skills. A trainer said:

> Women have got to recognize that the skills that they have are valuable; they devalue their feminine skills because they don't feel that they are important, but these are the skills that help them manage better because they help them avoid conflict and allow them to operate more collegially. They tend to value male skills, which might enable them to make decisions more

quickly, but this doesn't allow them to make decisions in the long term that are terribly meaningful.

We received comments on women's ability to manage because of their feminine qualities and perceptions. A feminine style, rather than the usual masculine one, was regarded as one relevant and successful in today's world.

This senior manager in Further Education argued forcefully that women's style was more effective:

> The style that is most natural to many women is the one that is more suitable to modern management styles than the old, hierarchical, dictatorial style of management. This has not been successful in the 1980's with new style companies, corporate devolved style of management. Words like love, family, atmosphere, feeling, reward now need to be used; these are things at the feminine end of the spectrum. They need to be incorporated into more successful management styles. Women are much more comfortable with that kind of management than men are.

This raises, of course, a number of questions, starting with the concept of 'natural' styles for women and men. Again, we should stress that it is more appropriate to discuss management styles as 'feminine' or 'masculine', remembering that women can – and do – manage within the masculine mould; and, at least in theory, there is no reason why men cannot manage in a feminine way. Large corporations seem willing to adapt their management styles and procedures, recognizing that this can be expected to increase productivity.

In our study, women spoke or wrote about specific areas where there appeared to be distinct differences between female and male styles and ways of working. They implied that the former style is more effective.

Ways of working – women and men

Paperwork

Several women in our project mentioned the different attitude to paperwork held by women and men:

> Men managers have to answer pieces of paper. Nothing is ever resolved in terms of how people feel about themselves.
> (Middle Manager in Teacher Training)

This woman believed that men feel secure with paperwork and hide behind it, dealing with and prioritizing paper rather than people. Her view was corroborated, although expressed slightly differently, by this head of a teachers' centre:

> One of the reasons why I have a bigger in-tray is because I spend a lot of time on my staff, the door is always open. Most of the male managers I have worked for get through their in-tray enormously quickly, I'm not saying they all do, but for many it forms a large part of what they do, whereas I spend more time with the punters and customers. I do the paperwork around the people, whereas the contrary is that you see the people around the paperwork.

Communication styles

There is a wealth of research to show that women and men use language differently (e.g. Lakoff, 1975; Scott, 1980; Spender, 1980; Skutnabb-Kangas, 1981). In defining variety in language, Skutnabb-Kangas notes not just regional, class-based, stylistic or situational variety but also sex-based and sex-conditioned variety. Scott details some of the differences, noting that women are more likely than men to use expressive language, to shy away from universal pronouncements, to use language that encourages community building and to be more polite. Women show respect for their audience by listening and remembering what has been said, giving signals of courtesy. Respect and support, shown by communication style, are better in management terms than men's stereotypical styles (Scott 1980). Dale Spender's findings are similar. Her analysis is from a more radical feminist perspective, and she places women's 'politeness' within the framework of expectations of the patriarchy.

Many women in our study remarked that, as managers, they were polite, tried to listen and allowed space for others to have a say. A principal in our study spoke of her willingness to listen to personal as well as professional matters from staff, believing that this is an attribute of a successful management. She commented too on her style of writing, saying she was careful to be friendly and jargon-free and always tried to avoid a patronizing tone.

Decision-making styles and dealing with conflict

Evidence suggests that women's decision-making styles tend to be more democratic and participatory than those of men. Women, notes Charol Shakeshaft, often use coalition building to achieve their goals. Women do not try to dominate discussion, thus they leave space for the participation of others. A primary school head in our survey agreed with this when she said:

> I am convinced that some women are less autocratic and more sympathetic than men. I don't believe in hanging on to power, such as it is. For example, I pass on circulars, post, letters, I try to keep the staff informed. I ask for help in making decisions and in solving problems.

Neuse (1978) suggests that women are less committed to formal hierarchy and more willing to submerge displays of personal power. They do this to encourage participation in the decision-making process. Many feminist researchers and practitioners today note that girls are more co-operative than boys in playing games and working in groups and that these co-operative skills will carry into the decision-making process when girls grow into women. This clearly has implications for the management styles of the future.

According to Charters and Jovick (1981) more participatory decision-making appears in female-managed schools. They reported that women are more likely than men to withdraw from confrontation and to use collaborative strategies. Men tend to use authoritarian responses. Women show greater respect for the dignity of teachers in their schools. As many more women than men see conflict as a negative state, ridding a school of conflict is more likely to occur with women in charge.

Our research findings confirm the above views:

> I don't wield power, I work on the consensus model, trying to achieve general agreement. I make day-to-day decisions, but major decisions are made by consensus. Papers are put forward for discussion, dates agreed for making decisions by . . . I have backed down, particularly from schemes of mine if we don't seem to be gaining consensus. You have to persuade people that schemes you have are a good idea, that's how any planning works. When dealing with conflicts I always try to look at the positive side, this may take half and hour, a day or longer. I have

only once stood out against clear opposition from the staff, about redeployment. This was because I felt as Head it was a job I had agreed to do and I should not duck this responsibility.

(Secondary Head)

Decisions are made democratically but I have a non-negotiable bottom line to do with equality and quality, rigour and high expectations, but within that framework everything is discussed. But the limit is very much to do with time and sometimes I have to make decisions based on some fairly cursory discussions with the Deputy Head.

(Primary Head)

An inspector described the collaborative decision-making process in a team of four women inspectors saying that there was discussion but no voting.

A headteacher described her frustrating attempts to manage openly and collaboratively. Her predecessor had been conflict-orientated and the staff were resistant to working in an alternative way. She said:

How can I get people to work collaboratively? There is such resistance. Everybody, including some of the management team seems caught up in the idea that these things don't work. I have been told that the troubles of the school lie at my door because I am too democratic, too soft.

Charters and Jovick argue that women and men handle conflict resolution differently, with women more likely to use collaborative strategies. This point was illustrated in our research. To our question 'How do you deal with conflict and contradiction?' we got a range of responses. Many women stressed the importance of letting people talk about problems and of listening intently, as noted previously:

It is very important to listen. People often create conflict because they feel that no-one takes notice of them, a bit like raising children. People want to be approved of, so I let them talk it through and try to recognize the feelings. Women are good at recognizing the feelings behind what is said, men always go straight for the issue. In staff grievances I listen and sometimes just to say 'I'm sorry , you obviously feel very hurt by what has happened' is enough, people just want you to recognize that their feelings are real.

(Senior woman in Higher Education)

I believe in discussions to solve problems, often letting people have their say and then trying to get them to compromise. I don't want people to feel that I am imposing on them.

(Head of Department)

Many of the women in our study, like those in the Charters and Jovick research, regarded conflict as a negative state, as something to be avoided:

I'm not confrontational, I want to appease the situation, so I am willing to make some compromises but not about principles. I try to do it by discussion.

(Further Education Lecturer)

I try to anticipate [conflict] and head it off, constantly review procedures that could lead to conflict, defuse with rational approach and with sympathy, be firm if you have to – in that order.

(Ex-head)

A senior teacher, however, thought that there were situations in which women could be accused of avoiding conflict:

Making generalizations, women managers are more efficient, delegate less and are prepared to work harder, push themselves harder. However, I feel they sometimes allow staff who are not fulfilling their obligations to continue to do so and don't challenge. They have a greater sensitivity and concern for the feelings of others, which can be misplaced.

One retired head was clear about her priorities – benefits to the children in her school over democratic process. Out and out conflict with her staff could have forced drastic action:

As a head, decisions were made after full consultation, discussion and by majority vote if necessary. I saw my role as a facilitator, but if I believed a decision was contrary to the interests of the children I would have opposed it. If the majority of staff had disagreed with me, I would have offered my resignation, but this never happened.

(Retired Head)

However, this was a contentious point, and a number of women challenged what they regarded as the stereotype of women avoiding conflict:

I think women can be very, very tough and are much more prepared to confront than men are, they are more open. I know that I can confront. I think I can also be very supportive to colleagues and that is what I think on the whole women are better about than men. I'm probably too aggressive at times, argue my case too strongly. I don't argue unless I am really convinced myself and have to be harshly attacked to recognize wrongness. One of the things that has helped me is to remember that we all have jobs because of children. If you constantly come back to that it helps in conflict.

(Advisory Teacher)

Towards change

A number of suggestions and strategies were mentioned by women in our study as ways forward. Training courses, conducting and publishing research, and consideration of the structures of organizations were three identifiable areas.

Training and courses for women managers, especially women-only courses, were seen by several women to be one way to advancement. Our reading showed that their views were shared. Many writers and researchers have argued that there is a need for women-only management courses (Hammond, 1986; Evans, 1987; Reavley, 1989). Agnew (1989) describes an in-service training course in Sheffield, which aimed to help women consider their career development and help them prepare for management positions. But some women in our study were less enthusiastic about the proliferation of training courses for women managers. A deputy head said:

> The training courses I have been on have superficially touched on the skills aspects of management. Yes, I did pick up some tips on my time management and stress management. I am now an expert on action planning! But the courses didn't touch on those REAL aspects – the power structures of education, the oppression we face, the way we are patronized and harassed – they didn't have any real political analysis. I mean, we are stuck here because of centuries of male oppression, not because there is a problem with the way we file our bits of paper.

Another woman wrote about a course that had:

> . . . helped me recognize just how skilled I am. But actually, it was the women I met at the course that made the real difference. The networking surpassed the course's written agenda.

We believe that if women-only courses are to be valuable they need to be considered in feminist ways, not in ways that blame women for imagined deficiencies. In the same way that girls are 'blamed' for their lack of success in maths and science, so are individual women managers 'blamed' for not managing like men. The system – androcentric and misogynist, is rarely challenged and without that challenge, the isolation of women in management continues to block advancement:

> Restructuring our preparation programmes to introduce feminist pedagogies and new methods of research and training are important steps, but, as the experience of women's studies indicates, they can have only marginal impact unless those who control the education profession – practitioners, policy-makers, and the professoriate – are willing to engage in a collaborative process through which both the professional and the institutions that support them are restructured to eliminate stratification based on gender.
>
> (Glazer, 1991, p. 338)

Published research – albeit in publications with a relatively small readership, can and do offer feminist analyses and alternatives. An example of this is *Outside of the norm: equity and management in educational institutions*: the report of a European Commission funded project of action research on equal opportunities 'race' and gender (Powney and Weiner, 1991). We believe there is a need for more books and articles charting the experience and work of women as teachers, educationalists and managers. We welcomed the growth of interest in women's experiences as documented in research we found, noticing an increase in the period between researching the dissertation and writing this book. Both by documenting practice and expounding theory, literature can have influence.

The roots of current debate on structures of organizations go back to earlier periods of feminist activity. In 1977 Kantner offered radical guidelines for reshaping organizations to make them more suitable places for women. She believes this can be achieved through relatively flat, decentralized companies in a structure which the majority of employees are arranged in project working teams. A deputy head from our sample stressed that structures did not have to be patriarchal:

> The ways women and men manage and use their personal power are different. Women are much more people orientated and have

different agendas. But models to avoid are those where decisions are never made and there is no structure. The anarchic approach is no good, you need structures and openness and consultation but the structures don't have to be patriarchal.

Her comment recalls Joreen Freeman's *The tyranny of structurelessness* (1973). This influential feminist article argued that if a group had no formal structure for decision-making, some individuals would become *de facto* leaders and that it was necessary to have structures to ensure everyone's involvement in decision-making.

An inspector interviewed in our survey spoke of the importance of getting the structure right in order to get things done. She believed that some structures, which passed as being democratic, were in fact disempowering rather than enabling. She also stressed the importance of talking about a feminist style of management rather than women as managers, echoing Marshall (1984). She elaborated on the qualities of a female manager. This inspector was one of the five women whose contribution forms Chapter 5 (see p. 87 for more on her views on management).

Taking a similar stance, a deputy head told us:

> Being a feminist manager implies you take care of everyone in your team, and acknowledge that they take care of you, too. Everyone's contribution is valuable. The team is important and I'm with them, not acting on them. I try to avoid the 'them' and 'us' split while being aware that my status and salary carries real responsibility. As a feminist, it is about my personal politics, too, and how I use that responsibility and power, both by networking and working in a creative, motivated and committed team.

Marshall notes that women have potential organizational models from the women's movement. Small groups linked in networks, possibly wider webs of networks linked in federations. Membership of small groups in this loose-knit organizational form is usually based on common interest. Typically, the aims would be providing emotional and professional support, sharing information and skills, pursuing new paths of personal and occupational development as a joint venture.

Working towards change was described in another way by Helen Regan. She outlined how she herself changed as she moved into the world of management and theorized on qualities.

She writes about the 'hard and soft qualities' of herself as a teacher/administrator, arguing that balancing the two are what makes for effective administration. The 'hard' qualities are those used in role-specific tasks; the 'soft' are those used in team-specific tasks. Recognizing the limitations of this polarity, she moves on to the pyramid metaphor. The top half equals the hard qualities. It is here that there is competition, an 'either/or' mode. Those in the top of the pyramid tend to be white males. In the bottom portion are the oppressed groups of society. There is a possibility for people to move up and gain wealth, status and power. It is the ability to move between the two that makes for good teaching, learning and administration. She uses the double helix metaphor, seeing this as inclusive, encompassing and legitimizing the 'either/or' and 'both/and' ways. She documents her own experience of recognizing and valuing complication and contradiction and subjectivity.

Our study gave us indications that some women are effecting change in British educational management. But we would be oversimplifying a complex situation and trivializing the obstacles facing women working within it if we concluded that there had been a major shift in attitudes towards women and female styles of management. Despite the recognition that women make excellent managers and that the female style of management is effective, Blackmore gives us evidence that the number of women in senior positions in education in Australia, Great Britain and the USA has decreased over the last fifteen years:

> The barriers facing women . . . can be summarized quite succinctly: women simply are not *good chaps*. (italics in original)
> (Hansard Society, 1990, p. 67)

Blackmore explains this re-emerging pattern of male dominance by exploring ways in which traditional masculinist views of management and leadership have dominated education and by noting the limitations of the liberal interventionist approach, characterized by Equal Opportunities policies. In her view it is the perception of leadership that is problematic, not women themselves – the displacement of women in organizational theory is derived from female invisibility or stereotyping in social and political theory, as we note in this dissertation. Blackmore recommends that feminists develop an alternative view of leadership and redefine it, using the accompanying power to act collectively. Her views coincide with the views of many of the women in our study. Management, she recommends, should look towards empowerment, not individual dominance or control, countering the emphasis on individualism, hierarchical relationships, bureaucratic rationality and abstract moral principles. Glazer expresses similar views:

> It would appear that the radical feminist slogan 'the personal is political' must be extended to 'the personal is professional' if women are to gain status in the public sphere. A feminised work force in the classroom and in the principal's office presents a challenging opportunity to strengthen the alliance between feminism and professionalism, restructuring the public and private spheres of human existence to be more responsive to women's concerns and to build nonbureaucratic, non-hierarchical systems.
>
> (Glazer, 1991, p. 338)

Stressing the need for resistance to 'masculinist notions of leadership' within educational management, feminists such as Hartsock, Blackmore, Spender, Glazer and ourselves believe in feminism as a better alternative:

> . . . [raising] for the first time the possibility of a fully human community, a community structured by its variety of direct relations among people, rather than their separation and opposition.
>
> (Hartsock, 1983, p. 262)

CHAPTER 8

Conclusion

In this conclusion we have extracted some of our main findings, noting some of the paradoxes that women face in education and educational management. Although we did not wish to provide a list of pointers for women to 'succeed' within educational management, we do, where we think relevant, make suggestions that women could use to help them survive and retain their vision of education despite the odds.

We set out to research aspects of the dynamics between feminism, power and educational management. Much of what we found, after completing the study, reading extensively and writing the dissertation and the book, confirmed our belief that change can and does occur when the manager is committed to working differently. That different way is seen by many – feminists and new management gurus – as a female way of working. We try here to summarize what we learnt from our research and readings and to indicate future possibilities.

The vast majority of women in our study believed that women manage differently from men. Many also believed that women manage better than men. Some women managers said or wrote that they consciously attempted to work in a feminist way seeking an alternative to a bureaucratic style. We found that co-operation and collaboration were words frequently used by women to describe their own management styles and aims. Yet women were aware of the contradictions inherent in challenging the hierarchical system from within and of other people's expectations of a manager and of managerial behaviour. Two senior women in Higher Education said that they had found themselves in conflict with the hierarchies in their institutions, which were antagonistic to their management styles. Senior women in schools told us of a 'bottom-up' resistance to collaborative management styles.

Women's skills were noted as being barely recognized and frequently devalued in society. Some women managers commented on their attempts to empower their women staff. They saw that they had a role in confidence building and encouraging others to recognize, value, develop and use their skills. Access to information was acknowledged as a crucial part of this empowering process. The term 'enabler' was used by some women to describe themselves as managers. This appears to be founded in a belief, expressed by others, for example Charol Shakeshaft, that power is not finite but expands as it is shared.

Giving responsibility and supporting staff may lead in the long-term to change. We believe, however, that delegating alone is not necessarily power-sharing or empowering. As it is in a linear model, delegation implies 'down', the shifting of a task to a deputy or subordinate. Combining responsibility with support and when necessary training is a more productive way forward. We recall ourselves the uncomfortable occasions when delegated to carry out a task without being given the necessary information and support.

Nearly all the women managers we interviewed felt that their experiences were different from those of male managers. The female experience in education, as elsewhere, is different from the male experience. We found that literature on management rarely describes the female experience – the assumption of the manager as male is still dominant. But articles and books on the experiences of women in management are now starting to appear. Some of these have a strong feminist perspective, others view women as the problem, suggesting techniques and strategies for being a successful woman in a man's world.

Many women had negative things to say about their own managers, both female and male. 'Women need to be tougher than men' is a frequently heard statement when women operate in a man's world. This can spill over into adopting some of the more obnoxious masculine styles of managing. We heard, and in particular received information from women that detailed the pain that bad management had caused them. This created additional stress, absenteeism, illness and in several cases women having to leave their jobs. We were horrified by the stories some women told us and moved by their strength of feeling and anger. There were women who commented on sexual and racial harassment from their line managers and the detrimental effect this had on their careers as well their self-esteem.

One factor that inhibits feminist and egalitarian ways of working is the hierarchical structure of education and the manager's role within it. The external structure is resistant to internal pressure. Despite opposition, poll tax capping, the Education Reform Act (in particular the National Curriculum, local management of schools, open enrolment and the abolition of the ILEA) and the Education White Paper have been imposed. Managers, even if they disagree, are legally obliged to implement these. Each impacts on people's working lives and learning.

Three-quarters of the women in our study were in senior positions, successful in the conventional.sense. Yet few women had career plans that paralleled a male model. We found that for some women, entering education *had* been a positive and deliberate choice but that the majority had drifted into their careers. The influence of families on choice of career was mentioned by a number of women. Some parents were teachers themselves; others saw the potential for their daughters to move into a middle-class profession. Even some women who were in influential and well-paid positions and whose careers looked to an outsider to have been planned, dispelled this myth. For these women, their careers had evolved around partners, children and other priorities and responsibilities. Many spoke of a holistic approach to their lives, of which career was one part.

Mothers mentioned the difficulties of childcare; of being made to feel guilty at spending time away from their children and of having to juggle personal and professional lives. A few mentioned caring male partners who took some responsibility for childcare but it was clear that childcare is still regarded as primarily a woman's issue. The pressure of working in education places women in a position where they are forced to devote more and more time to the job. Essential evening work – meetings, preparation and marking – leaves women with little time for relaxing/children, etc. It is ironic that teaching, seen as a 'good' job for working mothers, demands extremely long hours. As with so many things, the myth and the reality do not match. Yet not one woman in our study regretted having children and many told us of the positive aspects of being a mother.

Women's attitude towards power is ambivalent. Many in our study preferred the term 'influence' to power – not surprisingly as women often have negative experiences of being on the receiving end of power. Power, it seems, is both undesirable and desirable. There were feminists who told us of the need to empower women by a process of demystification and by removing the mythology surrounding it – many talked about empowering other women and their students. They discussed sharing power and working collaboratively and co-operatively.

Almost all the women in our study stated that they did not have professional power, recognizing that power is relative. Many women found personal power easier to acknowledge and felt happy with the power they had, consciously trying to use it in different, often feminist, ways. While many women who identified themselves as feminists did not feel they had much – in some cases any – power to make effective change in their places of work, they mentioned being strong and powerful in themselves and with other women. Perhaps personal power – 'power with others' – is more comfortable to acknowledge and is also more acceptable to feminists than professional power, commonly perceived as 'power over others'. Some women talked about their power in other areas. For example, they had a strong sense of their own worth and therefore power in women's groups and trade unions. In addition, some women spoke of the power of being middle-class with financial independence. Money and power are closely linked.

There were a few women in our study who had deliberately chosen not to apply for promotion – this was aligned variously to their radical class politics or their domestic priorities or to feminist principles. In this last group women talked about empowering pupils and students. For several women, this was feminist activism and a reason to stay in the classroom, school library, etc. and avoid becoming an administrator. This is not to imply that those women who had moved up the career structure devalued the work of the classroom teacher. Indeed they told us of their sense of loss at moving away from that depth of involvement with pupils and students. They told us, too, of the isolation they faced, particularly if they were trailblazers.

Our readings and research revealed that feminist teachers are faced with dilemmas. Options include:

- Staying in the classroom; avoiding promotion. This diminishes the compromises but also means having low status and wages. As feminists, do we want to perpetuate a system where the average woman earns just two-thirds of the average male wage?
- Ascending the career ladder and following male styles of management.
- Ascending the career ladder and adopting a more female style, recognizing the possible backlash.
- Leaving the profession but continuing to work for change in society, of which education is a part.
- Leaving the profession and prioritizing your personal life – potentially a radical alternative to the rat race.

Judi Marshall explains the dilemma thus, alluding to the liberal versus radical feminist debate:

> There are two broad alternatives open to me. I can set my sights on reform, accept the current male model of organisations and suggest that women survive within it. Or I can question basic assumptions, look to alternative women-centred value sources.
> (Marshall, 1984, p. 197)

Within education, there is a price, usually financial, to pay for staying at the base of the pyramid and a price to pay for moving up. It is unrealistic to suggest that a much higher salary will not involve making some unpleasant decisions and taking unpleasant action – such as having to make staff redundant.

From our research, we summarize suggestions made to improve the positions of women in education:

- implementation of equal opportunities policies;
- monitoring of selection procedures and policies;
- training of gatekeepers;
- equal access to management training and other INSET for women and men;
- mentoring for women;
- better childcare, maternity and paternity rights;
- developmental models of appraisal where both appraisers and appraisees have received training in equal opportunities;
- networking and women's support groups;
- positive action in recruiting. A quota system is one way of achieving this;
- equal opportunities interviewing.

While these suggestions may facilitate improvements for women in education, we remain sceptical of the idea that access alone equals equality; that equal numbers of women and men, without consideration of their roles, attitudes and behaviour, bring about significant change. There were feminists in our study who argued, too, that more radical restructuring, not only reforms, is needed.

The question 'What is a feminist?' has no single answer. No two self-definitions from women in our study were identical, although most identified themselves as feminists. This identification was not surprising, given our selection of women to interview and our choice of journals for advertisements. For many, feminism was central to their lives and understanding of the world, as it is to us. The limitations of white middle-class feminism were recognized and often commented on. Among those women who did not describe themselves as feminists there was a range of views, too, and some described themselves as ex-feminists or post-feminists. Other women disliked the connotations of the word 'feminism' while still holding a woman-centred perspective.

Almost all the women in our study acknowledged the role that gender played in their personal and professional lives. For the feminists, analysis of gender took place within the structures of patriarchy. There was a clear recognition of the impact that gender has on learning, teaching and managing.

What we found, then, were contradictions, paradoxes and chimera. We see a contradiction between being a feminist and being a manager in education today, although not between being a feminist and working with a feminist management style. There is an inherent contradiction between maintaining feminist principles and holding a powerful position in a linear hierarchy. A manager, by definition, is in a high position on the linear scale. Feminism is wary of pyramidal and linear models and looks to alternatives to hierarchies, to providing multi-dimensional ways of working. We stress that acknowledging this contradiction does not imply that the two are mutually exclusive; that women who become senior managers are not or cannot be feminists. Many women in our study were committed, active feminists who held high positions in educational management. We recognize the contradiction as an example of conflicts and tensions experienced by many women.

Paradoxically, current trends in management outside the education system are extolling the values of a different and female way of working. Good management is now seen as valuing collaboration and consultation, power sharing, team building, prioritizing and praising staff, caring for the physical environment, a holistic approach, flexibility and good listening skills. Moves away from formalistic towards participative models could mean advancement for women. Although education is emulating big business in terms of language and concepts, as yet the current trends in commerce and industry towards a so-called female style of management have not had an impact on the male hierarchy in education.

The abolition of the ILEA revealed another paradox. On the one hand it removed a powerful educational body, which was often regarded as a forerunner in equality work in education. On the other, the proliferation of posts in the new LEAs in London opened up some career possibilities for black and white women and black men. Three issues complicate this: (i) these jobs are continually under threat; (ii) we have seen the new London local education authorities set up and working in ways that limit autonomy, increasingly governed by accountability, finance and functionalism; and (iii) LEAs themselves are under threat from central government; their power and functions are diminishing as schools opt out.

We found working together on the research, dissertation and book has affected our personal and professional lives (although we recognize that this is a problematic distinction). The non-hierarchical way we have worked has been in contrast to the climate of education in the late 1980s and early 1990s. We found working closely and collectively an example we can use when working with other women. It is a method that fascinated other women. We gained insights into common and contradictory experiences of a wide range of women and have learnt much from the women in our study. From many points of view, the work was a real learning experience – the interviews, the readings, the discussion, the process of working together, the influence of women researched and of each other. It gave us skills in management we do not think we would have got from a course that focused exclusively on management without taking into account a wider socio-political context. The work also gave us confidence in ourselves and increased our ability to deal with our managers. It helped us clarify issues around career decisions. We felt empowered by our increased knowledge of theory and research.

We continue to explore issues of power, feminism and educational management. In this book we have written about these issues and have documented experiences of a number of women. Significantly, we did this by working together in an experimental way. It was an enormous amount of hard work; there was also a lot of laughter, good food and real enjoyment.

Appendix 1

Statistical information

Interviews

Requests for interview	60
Interviews conducted	44
Declined to be interviewed	2
Unable to arrange interview but completed questionnaire	6
Unable to arrange interview and did not return questionnaire	6
Did not respond	2
Response rate	96%

Questionnaires

Number sent	54.0
Number returned	30.0
Response rate	55.5%

Letters

Number received	11

Profile Sheets (see Appendix 2)

Number completed	71
Declined to complete the sheets	3
Response rate	96%

(Note that women who sent letters did not complete profile sheets)

Information from the profile sheets: a summary

Posts
Fifty-one women (73 per cent) were in senior posts. (We have interpreted this to be a position from head of department, to deputy head
or head, to senior executive/manager in local education authority
or higher education. Women in our study were from all phases in
education). Three women had retired from senior posts. Four women
had left education; one to become a financial adviser; two to have
children and one to practise as a therapist.

Salaries

Salary (£000s)	Number	Percentage
Over £40	1	1.5
31–35	4	5.0
26–30	13	19.5
21–25	24	35.5
16–20	15	20.0
11–15	4	5.0
Under 11*	9	12.0
Undisclosed (senior woman in H.E.)	1	1.5

* Two of these women were main professional grade (MPG) teachers, one was a
researcher, the others were in part-time employment, pensioned or unemployed.

Benefits
One woman had an official car allowance and health insurance. All
inspectors and advisers had a car/mileage allowance.

Position in family
Forty-three (62 per cent) were either first-born or only children. Of
the women in senior positions, 52 per cent were first-born or only
children. Of the women in junior positions, 14 per cent were first-
born or only children.

Appendix 2

Quantitative information and self-descriptions: a summary

Age	Post	Salary (£ 000s)	Position in family	Self-description
20–25	Teacher	7–10	Youngest	Jewish, female, British, left wing, middle-class
26–30	Adviser	21–25	Only child	Black woman
26–30	Teacher	11–15	Only child	Working-class woman
31–35	Senior Lecturer	16–20	Eldest	Black, Afro-Caribbean
31–35	Lecturer	11–15	Eldest	Working-class, British, heterosexual but like women more than men
31–35	School's Industry Co-ordinator	16–20	Only child	Working-class at birth, middle-class life now
31–35	Head of Department	16–20	Eldest	Middle-class, white, heterosexual
31–35	Advisory Teacher	21–25	Eldest	A woman
31–35	Deputy Head	21–25	Eldest	Originally working-class, lesbian, white
31–35	Inspector	26–30	Eldest	European – woman
31–35	Senior Lecturer	21–25	Eldest	British of Afro-Caribbean descent. Middle-class

Age	Post	Salary (£ 000s)	Position in family	Self-description
31–35	Inspector	21–25	Youngest	Black – Punjabi. Born in an upper-class family, expelled from Uganda – downward social mobility. Politically committed to equality – supporting working-class interests
31–35	Teacher	7–10	Fifth	English woman, working to middle-class
36–40	Head of Basic Education	16–20	Eldest	Polish, middle-class via education and present life-style
36–40	Deputy Head	21–25	Fourth born	Afro-Caribbean – working-class
36–40	Deputy Head	21–25	Youngest	White, able-bodied, heterosexual, middle-class. I would describe myself as a struggling woman in a male society
36–40	Advisory Teacher	16–20	Middle	Irish woman, heterosexual, working-class origins
36–40	Head of Unit	16–20	Eldest	White, middle-class, heterosexual woman
36–40	Senior Inspector	31–35	Only child	White, middle-class in origin, middle-class in reality, co-parent, lesbian, home owner and consumer
36–40	Inspector	21–25	Second born	A black woman from a black working-class background
36–40	Development Officer	21–25	Eldest	Able-bodied, white, middle-class, heterosexual, socialist

Age	Post	Salary (£ 000s)	Position in family	Self-description
36–40	Headteacher	21–25	Eldest	Middle-class, white, differently-abled, heterosexual
36–40	Head of Teachers' Centre	21–25	Third born	White, middle-class
36–40	Financial Adviser	21–25	Eldest	Middle-class, British
36–40	Senior Teacher	16–20	Youngest	White, English, middle-class
36–40	Advisory Teacher	16–20	Eldest	White, able-bodied, middle-class with working-class roots, heterosexual
36–40	Inspector	26–30	Second born	From a northern working-class background
36–40	Executive Director	31–35	Third born	Lower middle-class – heterosexual
36–40	Part-time Primary Teacher	7–10	Eldest	White, able-bodied (currently) lesbian – feminist
36–40	Advisory Teacher	21–25	Eldest	English, black, able, heterosexual, classless
36–40	Librarian	21–25	Eldest	Welsh, heterosexual, lower-middle-class
36–40	Teacher	11–15	Second born	White, British, heterosexual, lower-middle-class
36–40	TVEI Adviser	26–30	Only child	White, middle-class
36–40	Researcher and Lecturer	7–10	Eldest	White, middle-class, Jewish by birth and culture but not practising religion, heterosexual
36–40	Education Counsellor	7–10	Third born	Quite cultured, able-bodied and able-minded, white Caucasian, heterosexual and aspiring working-class

Age	Post	Salary (£ 000s)	Position in family	Self-description
41–45	Inspector	21–25	Third born	Culture – an amalgam of Indian, South African and English. Able-bodied. Race – irrelevant as I don't ascribe to this concept. Heterosexual. Class – complicated by racism both in South Africa and Britain
41–45	Divisional Adult Education Principal	21–25	Eldest	White, Welsh, working-class raised
41–45	Teacher	7–10	Only child	Scottish, European, heterosexual, working-class
41–45	Advisory Teacher	21–25	Eldest	White, middle-class
41–45	Housewife and mother	–	Second born	Working-class, widely read
41–45	Headteacher	31–35	Second born	Working-class background, middle-class lifestyle, white, European, heterosexual
41–45	Senior Inspector	26–30	Eldest	[Not completed]
41–45	Project Co-ordinator	21–25	Youngest	White, currently lesbian, able-bodied, working-class roots
41–45	Librarian	16–20	Second born	White, political lesbian
41–45	Head of Department	21–25	Only child	Middle-class of working-class roots, white, heterosexual
41–45	Headteacher	26–30	Second born	White, middle-class, heterosexual, advantaged
41–45	Headteacher	26–30	Second born	Was working-class – northern up-bringing, now

Age	Post	Salary (£ 000s)	Position in family	Self-description
41–45	Vice-Principal	31–34	Eldest	middle-class by education and background Working-class by origins, NUM scholarship to university. Variable sexuality. Now an older parent of a young daughter in a non-traditional relationship
41–45	Senior Adviser	26–30	Eldest	Jewish, white heterosexual, middle-class, able bodied
41–45	Head of Department	26–30	Second born	Jewish, middle-class, heterosexual
41–45	Deputy Head	21–25	Only child	[Not completed]
41–45	Senior Inspector	26–30	Eldest	White, heterosexual, middle-class, able-bodied, small
41–45	Media Resources Officer	16–20	Eldest	White, middle-class, able-bodied, lesbian
41–45	Professor	21–25	Eldest	Educated working-class woman
41–45	Head of Department	16–20	Eldest	Lesbian, moved up to middle-class
46–50	Lecturer	16–20	Eldest	Agnostic, Jewish, feminist, radical politics
46–50	Senior Lecturer	21–25	Only child	[Not completed]
46–50	Unemployed	–	Eldest	White Australian, working-class
46–50	Senior post in Higher Education	–	Eldest	White, female, middle-class
46–50	Senior Inspector	26–30	Second born	Anti-racist feminist, able-bodied but diminishing . . .
46–50	Lecturer	21–25	Only child	Lesbian, able-bodied, white

Age	Post	Salary (£ 000s)	Position in family	Self-description
46–50	Teacher	16–20	Eldest	Entirely able-bodied but creaking at the joints. Of European origin. Heterosexual
46–50	Further Education Co-ordinator	21–25	Eldest	White, disabled, working-class woman made good
46–50	Head of Teachers' Centre	26–30	Second born	White, middle-class from working-class background, heterosexual
51–55	Senior post in Higher Education	26–30	Only child	Jewish, female, middle-class, diabetic
51–55	Head of Department	16–20	Only child	Middle-class, slightly above average in ability, married with two children – both graduates
51–55	Self employed therapist	16–20	Second born	[Long objection to the question]
55–60	Senior post in Higher Education	41 plus	Second born	White female
61–65	Retired Head	–	Only child	White, Jewish, working-class origin, heterosexual
61–65	Retired Deputy	–	Youngest	[Not completed]
61–65	District Inspector	26–30	Eldest	Middle-class, Anglo-Saxon, white, heterosexual

Appendix 3

Interview guidelines

Confidential

Note:
- everything is confidential;
- the report will preserve your anonymity;
- you need not answer all the questions;
- you may answer the questions in any order;
- your answers can be as long – or as short – as you like.

Education and career pattern

Describe your career and education (including qualifications) from leaving school, indicating number of years at each stage.

Why did you go into education? How would you describe your career pattern to date? Was it 'drift' or luck?

Have there been obstacles to your chosen career development? If yes, could you describe them and say what strategies you used?

Have you had/got mentors?
Sponsorship/and patronage?

Lifestyle and family

What education did your mother (and/or other adult women of significance in your childhood – aunts, grandmothers, friends) have?

What education did your father (and/or other adult men of significance in your childhood – uncles, grandfathers, friends) have?

Siblings – is their career pattern/education like or unlike yours?

Domestic/personal situation

Would you like to say anything about support in your life?

What effect do you think having children (or not) and/or being a carer has on a woman's career?

If you would like to say anything about your own situation please do.

Feminism

Do you describe yourself as a feminist?

What does feminism mean to you?

Is there a tension between your career pattern, your position and feminism?

Do your colleagues describe you as a feminist? (compliment or insult?) Specify: female and male colleagues.

Power

Briefly describe your job, saying what issues of power are in it for you (i.e. your own power/lack of power; structural power. Do you believe you have any real power in your job?)

Would you like to relate this to issues of oppression?

Has your job lived up to your expectations in terms of the power you have to effect change?

Power in other areas relevant to you, e.g. politics, community involvement and activities?

How do you see yourself as able to effect change? How does the structure of the institution affect this? Are there contradictions?

Management and your job

How are decisions made in your institution/place of work? What is your role?

Would you like to say something about women as managers?

Do you think there is a style difference between female and male managers?
  Do you want to say anything about your current line manager?
  If relevant, please say something about yourself as a manager.

Do you work fixed hours? Does your professional time encroach on your private time? If yes, is there a cut-off point?

Do you want to say anything about dress codes in your job?

Gender issues in work relations

Could you describe your relationship with:

• colleagues (women and men);
• pupils and students (girls and boys).

The future

Where would you like to go?

Anything else?

Appendix 4

Profile sheet

Confidential

It would be useful to us if you would fill in this section. It will help us to establish a profile of women in this study as well as explore the relationships between aspects of peoples' lives and experience.

Your responses will be kept both anonymous and strictly confidential.
Please remember that you need not not answer all the questions.

Name

Post/position

Salary
(please circle)   7–10K   11–15K   16–20K   21–25K
                              26–30K   31–35K   36–40K   41K +
(and indicate any other benefits, e.g. car allowance; health schemes, etc.)

Age
(please circle)   20–25   26–30   31–35   36–40
                              41–45   46–50   51–55   56–60
                              61–65   66–70

Position in family (e.g. eldest child; only daughter with four brothers)

How do you describe yourself? (in terms of culture, differently abled, ethnicity, race, sexuality, social class)

Thank you for your co-operation and time.

Bibliography

Acker, S. (1983) 'Women and teaching: a semi-detached sociology of a semi-profession', in S. Walker, and L. Barton (eds) *Gender, Class and Education*. Lewes, Falmer.

Acker, S. (ed.) (1989) *Teachers, Gender and Careers*. Lewes, Falmer.

Adams, C. (1991) 'Women Chief Education Officers don't have to forego families', *Times Educational Supplement*, 26 April, 19.

Agnew, D. (1989) 'A world of women: an approach to personal and career development for women teachers in primary schools', in H. De Lyon and F. Widdowson-Migniuolo (eds) *Women Teachers: Issues and Experiences*. Milton Keynes, Open University Press.

Al-Khalifa, E. (1989) 'Management by halves: women teachers and school management', in H. De Lyon and F. Widdowson Migniuolo (eds) *Women Teachers: Issues and Experiences*. Milton Keynes, Open University Press.

Anthias, F. and Yuval-Davis, N. (1983) 'Contextualizing feminism – gender, ethnic and class divisions', *Feminist Review*, 15, 62–75.

Ball, S. (1987) *The Micropolitics of the School: Towards a Theory of School Organisation*. London, Methuen.

Barrett, M. (1987) 'Gender and class: Marxist perspectives on education', in M. Arnot and G. Weiner (eds) *Gender and the Politics of Schooling*. London, Hutchinson.

Bell, C. and Newby, H. (eds) (1977) *Doing Sociological Research*. London, Allen and Unwin.

Berger, J. (1972) *Ways of Seeing*. London, BBC.

Blackmore, J. (1989) 'Educational leadership: a feminist critique and reconstruction', in J. Smyth (ed.) *Critical Perspectives on Educational Leadership*. Lewes, Falmer.

Blake, P.R. and Moulton, J.S. (1964) *The Managerial Grid*. Houston, TX, Gulf Publishing Company.

Brownmiller, S. (1984) *Femininity*. London, Simon and Schuster.

Bryce, L. (1989) *The Influential Woman: How to Achieve Success Without Losing your Femininity*. London, Arrow.

Bunch, C. (1979) 'Not by degrees: feminist theory and education', in C. Bunch and S. Pollack (eds) (1983) *Learning Our Way: Essays in Feminist Education*. New York, Crossing Wall.

Burgess, H. (1989) 'A sort of career: women in primary schools', in C. Skelton (ed.) *Whatever Happens to Little Women? Gender and Primary Schooling*. Milton Keynes, Open University Press.

Bush, T. (1989) 'The nature of theory in educational management', in T. Bush (ed.) *Managing Education: Theory and Practice*. Milton Keynes, Open University Press.

Byrne, E.M. (1987) 'Education for equality', in M. Arnot and G. Weiner (eds) *Gender and the Politics of Schooling*. London, Hutchinson.

Cameron, J. (1990) *The Competitive Woman*. London, Mercury.

Carby, H. (1982) 'White women listen! Black feminism and the boundaries of sisterhood', in *The Empire Strikes Back: Race and Racism in 70's Britain*. London, Centre for Contemporary Cultural Studies/Hutchinson.

Carpenter, L. (1989) 'A discourse on the care and handling of feminist administrators', *Feminist Teacher*, 4 (2/3), 43–5.

Chapkis, W. (1986) *Beauty Secrets*. London, Women's Press.

Charters, W.W. and Jovick, T.D. (1981) 'The gender of principals and principal/teacher relations in elementary schools', in P. Schmuck, W. Charters and R. Carlson (eds) *Educational Policy and Management*. New York, Academic Press.

Cohen, L. and Manion, L. (1989) *Research Methods in Education* (3rd edn). London, Routledge.

Cohen, D.C. and March, J. (1989) 'Leadership and ambiguity', in T. Bush (ed.) *Managing Education: Theory and Practice*. Milton Keynes, Open University Press.

Coulson, A.A. (1987) 'Recruitment and management development for primary headship', in G. Southworth (ed.) *Reading in Primary School Management*. Lewes, Falmer.

Darking, L. (1991) 'The equalisers', *Times Educational Supplement*, 3 May, 18.

Davidson, H. (1985) 'Unfriendly myths about women teachers', in J. Whyte, *et al*. (eds) *Girl Friendly Schooling*. London, Methuen.

Davies, J.L. and Morgan, A. (1989) 'Management of higher education institutions in a period of contraction and uncertainty', in T. Bush (ed.) *Managing Education: Theory and Practice*. Milton Keynes, Open University Press.

de Beauvoir, S. (1953) *The Second Sex*. London, Cape.

De Lauretis, T. (1990) 'Eccentric subjects: feminist theory and historical consciousness', *Feminist Studies*, 16(1), 115–50.

Department of Education and Science (1983) *Circular 3/83*. London, HMSO.

Department of Education and Science (1991) *Statistics of Education: Teachers in England and Wales 1990*. London, HMSO.

Department of Education and Science (1991) *Education Statistics for the UK, 1990*. London, HMSO.

Department of Education and Science (1991) Statistical bulletin 18/91. London, HMSO.

Dinnerstein, D. (1978) *The Rocking of the Cradle and the Ruling of the World*. London, Souvenir Press.

Dix, L. (1990) *A Chance for the Top: The Lives of Women Business Graduates*. London, Transworld.

Du Bois, B. (1983) 'Passionate scholarship: notes on values, knowing and method in feminist social science', in G. Bowles and R. Duelli Klein (eds) *Theories of Women's Studies*. London, Routledge and Kegan Paul.

Dyhouse, C. (1981) *Girls Growing up in Late Victorian and Edwardian England*. London, Routledge and Kegan Paul.

Eichler, M. (1988) *Nonsexist Research Methods: A Practical Guide*. Boston, MA, Allen and Unwin.

Eisenstein, Z.R. (1986) *The Radical Future of Liberal Feminism*. Boston, MA, Northeastern University Press.

Elshtain, J.B. (1981) *Public Man/Private Woman*. Princeton, Princeton University Press.

Evans, J. (1987) 'The benefits of women only courses in management', *Transition*, 16–17.

Everard, K.B. and Morris, G. (1990) *Effective School Management* (2nd edn). London, Harper and Row.

Evetts, J. (1987) 'Becoming career ambitious: the career strategies of married women who became primary headteachers in the 1960s and 1970s', *Educational Review*, 39(1), 15–29.

Evetts, J. (1988) 'Returning to teaching: the career breaks and returns of married women primary headteachers', *British Journal of Sociology of Education*, 9(1), 81–96.

Evetts, J. (1989) 'Married women and career: career history accounts of primary headteachers', *Qualitative Studies in Education*, 2(2), 89–105.

Fiedler, F. (1967) *A Theory of Leadership Effectiveness*. New York, Mcgraw Hill.

Firestone, S. (1971) *The Dialectic of Sex: The Case of Feminist Revolution*. London, Cape.

Forrest, A. (1989) 'Women in a man's world', *Journal of Management Development*, 8(6), 61–9.

Freeman, J. (1973) 'The tyranny of structurelessness', in A. Koedt,

E. Levine and A. Rapone (eds) *Radical Feminism*. New York, Quadrangle Books.

French, M. (1985) *Beyond Power: On Women, Men and Morals*. London, Cape.

Friedan, B. (1965) *The Feminine Mystique*. London, Cape.

Fritchie, R. (1987) 'Process, Mary, task Harry?', *Women and Training News*, 28, 4.

Getzels, J. and Gubas, E. (1954) 'The structure of roles and role conflict in the teaching situation', *Journal of Educational Sociology*, 29(1), 30–40.

Gilligan, C. (1982) *In a Different Voice: Psychological Theory and Women's Development*. Cambridge, MA, Harvard University Press.

Glazer, J.S. (1991) 'Feminism and professionalism in teaching and educational administration', *Educational Administration Quarterly*, 27(3), 321–42.

Grant, R. (1987) 'A career in teaching: a survey of middle school teachers' perceptions with particular reference to the career of women teachers', *British Educational Research Journal*, 13(3), 227–39.

Grant, R. (1989a) 'Heading for the top: the career experiences of a group of women deputies in one LEA', *Gender and Education*, 1(2), 113–25.

Grant, R. (1989b) 'Women teachers career pathways: towards an alternative model of "career"', in S. Acker (ed.) *Teachers, Gender and Careers*. Lewes, Falmer.

Gray, H.L. (1989) 'Gender considerations in school management: masculine and feminine leadership styles', in C. Riches and M. Morgan (eds) *Human Resource Management in Education*. Milton Keynes, Open University Press.

Greer, G. (1970) *The Female Eunuch*. London, MacGibbon and Kee.

Halpin, A.W. and Winer, B.J. (1957) 'A factorial study of the leadership behavior descriptions', in R.M. Stogdill and A.E. Coons (eds) *Leader Behavior: Its Description and Measurement*. Columbus, Ohio State University.

Hammond, V. (1986) 'Women in management from platitudes to action', *Transition*, 23–5.

Hansard Society. (1990) *Women at the Top: Report of the Commission*. London, The Hansard Society.

Harding, S. (ed.) (1987) *Feminism and Methodology: Social Science Issues*. Milton Keynes, Open University Press.

Hart, L. (1989) 'Women in primary management', in C. Skelton (ed.) *Whatever Happens to Little Women? Gender and Primary Schooling*. Milton Keynes, Open University Press.

Hartsock, N. (1983) *Money, Sex and Power: Towards a Feminist Historical Materialism*. New York, Longman.

Hearn, J. (ed.) (1989) *The Sexuality of Organisations*. London, Sage.

Hennig, M. and Jardim, A. (1979) *The Managerial Woman*. London, Pan.

Hooks, B. (1981) *Ain't I a Woman? Black Women and Feminism*. London, Pluto.

Hoyle, E. (1982) 'The micropolitics of educational organisations', *Education Management and Administration*, 10(2), 87–98.

Hughes, M., Ribbins, P. and Thomas, H. (eds) (1985) *Managing Education: the System and the Institution*. London, Cassell.

ILEA (1984) *Teachers on Maternity Leave*. RS921/84. London, ILEA.

ILEA (1987) *Women Teachers in Birmingham*. London, ILEA.

ILEA (1989) *Reluctant Masters: Essays by Fifteen Women on the Open University MA in Education Gender and Education module 1988*. London, ILEA.

ILEA (1990) *Women in Management: A Positive Approach*. London, ILEA.

Jayne, E. (1989) 'Women as leaders of schools: the role of training', *Educational Management and Administration*, 17, 109–14.

Jeffreys, S. (1990) *Anti-climax*. London, Women's Press.

Johnson, S. (1792) 'Letters to Dr Taylor', in R. W. Chapman (ed.) (1952) *Letters of Samuel Johnson*, 1, Oxford, Clarendon Press.

Jones, A. (1987) *Leadership for Tomorrow's Schools*. Oxford, Blackwells.

Jones, M. L. (1990) 'The attitudes of men and women primary school teachers to promotion and education management', *Educational Management and Administration*, 18(3), 11–16.

Jones, C. and Mahony, P. (eds) (1989) *Learning our Lines: Sexuality and Social Control in Education*. London, Women's Press.

Josefowitz, N. (1980) *Paths to Power: A Woman's Guide from First Job to Top Executive*. London, Columbus.

Joseph, K. (1983) 'Raw deal for girls draws fire from Sir Keith', *Times Educational Supplement*, 18 November, 6.

Kantner, R. M. (1977) *Men and Women of the Corporation*. New York, Basic Books.

Kayofski, H. (1990) 'The female revolution', *Wave*, November, 27–31.

Kelly, A. (1978) 'Feminism and research', *Women's Studies International Quarterly*, 1, 225–32.

Klein, R. Duelli. (1983) 'How to do what we want to do: thought about feminist methodology', in G. Bowles and R. Duelli Klein (eds) *Theories of Women's Studies*. London, Routledge and Kegan Paul.

Korabik, K. and Ayman, R. (1989) 'Should women managers have to act like men?', *Journal of Management Development*, 8(6), 23–32.

Kuhn, T. (1962) *The Structure of Scientific Revolutions*. Chicago, University of Chicago Press.

Kuhn, A. and Wolpe, A.M. (eds) (1978) *Feminism and Materialism: Women and Modes of Production*. London, Routledge and Kegan Paul.

Lakoff, R. (1975) *Language and Women's Place*. New York, Harper and Row.

Lambert, P. (1989) 'Women into educational management', *Adults Learning*, 1(4), 106.

Leonard, R. (1981) 'Managerial styles in academe: do women and men differ?' Paper presented at the meeting of Southern Speech Communication Association, Austin, TX.

Lorde, A. (1983) 'There is no hierarchy of oppressions', *Interracial Books for Children Bulletin*, 14(3/4), 3.

Lyons, N. (1983) 'Two perspectives on self, relationships and morality', *Harvard Educational Review*, 53(2), 124–5.

Maguire, A. (1985) 'Power: now you see it, now you don't. A woman's guide to how power works', in L. Steiner-Scott (ed.) *Personally Speaking: Women's Thoughts on Women's Issues*. Dublin, Attic.

Mahony, P. (1985) *Schools for the Boys: Co-education Re-assessed*. London, Women's Press.

Marshall, J. (1984) *Women Managers: Travellers in a Male World*. Chichester, Wiley.

Marshall, C. (1985) 'From culturally defined to self-defined: career stages for women administrators', *Journal of Educational Thought*, 19(2), 134–47.

Martinez, Z.N. (1988) 'From a representational to a holographic paradigm: the emergence of female power', *Atlantis*, 14, 134–40.

Maslow, A.H. (1943) 'A theory of human motivation', *Psychological Review*, 50, 370–96.

Massengill, D. and Di Marco, N. (1979) 'Sex role stereotypes and requisite management characteristics: a current replication', *Sex Roles*, 5(5), 5–10.

Maw, J. *et al.* (1984) *Education Plc?* London, Institute of Education.

Middleton, S. (1984) 'The sociology of women's education as a field of academic study', in M. Arnot and G. Weiner (eds) (1987) *Gender and the Politics of Schooling*. London, Hutchinson.

Middleton, S. (1989) 'Educating feminists: a life history study', in S. Acker (ed.) *Teachers, Gender and Careers*. Lewes, Falmer.

Mies, M. (1983) 'Towards a methodology for feminist research', in G. Bowles and R. Duelli Klein (eds) *Theories of Women's Studies*. London, Routledge and Kegan Paul.

Minhas, R. (1986) 'Race, sex and class: making the connections', in ILEA Primary Matters. London, ILEA.

Mintzberg H. (1973) *The Nature of Managerial Work*. New York, Harper and Row.

Mitchell, J. (1971) *Women's Estate*. New York, Bantam.

Mitchell, J. (1974) *Psychoanalysis and Feminism*. New York, Vintage.

Mitchell, J. and Oakley, A. (eds) (1987) *What is Feminism?* Oxford, Blackwell.

Morgan, G. (1986) *Images of Organisation*. London, Sage.

Morgan, R. (1989) *The Demon Lover: On the Sexuality of Terrorism*. London, Methuen.

Morglen, H. (1983) 'Power and empowerment', in R. L. Dudovitz, (ed.) *Women in Academe*. Oxford, Pergamon.

Mortimore, P. and Mortimore, J. (eds) (1991) *The Secondary Head: Roles Responsibilities and Reflections*. London, PCP.

Murphy, L. and Livingstone, J. (1985) 'Racism and the limits of radical feminism', *Race and Class*, 26(4), 61–70.

Myers, K. (ed.) (1992) *Genderwatch 11: after the ERA. Self-assessment Schedules for Use in Schools*. Cambridge, Cambridge University Press.

Neuse, S. (1978) 'Professionalism and authority: women in public service', *Public Administrative Review*, 38, 436–41.

Newman, J. (1991) 'Enterprising women: images of success', in S. Franklin, C. Lury and J. Stacey (eds) *Off-centre: Feminism and Cultural Studies*. London, Harper Collins.

Nielsen, J. (ed.) (1990) *Feminist Research Methods: Exemplary Readings in the Social Sciences*, Boulder, CO, Westview Press.

Oakley, A. (1981) 'Interviewing women: a contradiction in terms', in H. Roberts (ed.) *Doing Feminist Research*. London, Routledge and Kegan Paul.

O'Brien, M. (1986) 'Feminism and the politics of education', *Interchange*, 17(2), 91–105.

Ostriker, A. (1987) *Stealing the Language: The Emergence of Women's Poetry in America*. London, Women's Press.

Piercy, M. (1982) *Woman on the Edge of Time*. London, Women's Press.

Pitner, N. J. (1981) 'Hormones or harems: are the acts of superintending different for women?' in P. Schmuck, W. Charters and R. Carlson (eds) *Educational Policy and Management*. New York, Academic Press.

Powney, J. and Weiner, G. (1991) *Outside of the Norm: Equity and Management in Educational Institutions*. European Commission funded report, unpublished.

Raymond, J. (1986) *A Passion for Friends: Towards a Philosophy of Female Affection*. London, Women's Press.

Reavley, M. (1989) 'Who needs training – women or organisations?', *Journal of Management Development*, 8(6).

Regan, H. (1990) 'Not for women only: school administration as a feminist activity', *Teachers College Record*, 91(4), 565–77.

Rich, A. (1976) *Of Woman Born: Motherhood as Experience and Institution*. New York, Bantam.

Roberts, H. (ed.) (1981) *Doing Feminist Research*. London, Routledge and Kegan Paul.

Schein, V.E. (1976) 'Think manager – think male', *The Atlanta Economic Review*, March–April.

Schniedewind, N. (1983) 'Feminist values: guidelines for a teaching methodology in women's studies', in C. Bunch and S. Pollack (eds) *Learning Our Way: Essays in Feminist Education*. New York, Crossing Wall.

Scott, K.P. (1980) 'Perceptions of communication competence: what's good for the goose is not good for the gander', in *Women's Studies International Quarterly*, 3(2/3), 199–208.

Scott, S. (1985) 'Feminist research and qualitative methods: a discussion of some of the issues', in R.G. Burgess (ed.) *Issues in Educational Research and Qualitative Methods*. Brighton, Falmer.

Segerman-Peck, L.M. (1991) *Networking and Mentoring: A Woman's Guide*. London, Piatkus.

Shakeshaft, C. (1987) *Women in Educational Administration*. Newbury Park, CA, Sage.

Sheppard, D.L. (1989) 'Organisations, power and sexuality: the image and self image of women managers', in J. Hearn, *et al.* (eds) *The Sexuality of Organisations*. London, Sage.

Shipman, M.D. (ed.) (1985) *Educational Research: Principles, Policies and Practices*. Lewes, Falmer.

Shipman, M.D. (1988) *The Limitation of Social Research* (3rd edn). London, Longman.

Shipman, M.D. (1990) *In Search of Learning: A New Approach to School Management*. Oxford, Blackwell.

Sikes, P. (1985) 'The life cycle of the teacher', in S. Ball and I. Goodman (eds) *Teachers' Lives and Careers*. Lewes, Falmer.

Simeone, A. (1987) *Academic Women: Working Towards Equality*. South Hadley, MA, Bergin and Garvey.

Singer, L. (1987) 'Value, power and gender: do we need a different voice?' in J. Genova (ed.) *Power, Gender, Values*. Edmonton, Alberta, Academic Press.

Skutnabb-Kangas, T. (1981) *Bilingualism or Not?* Clevedon, Avon, Multilingual Matters.

Smith, D.E. (1988) *The Everyday World as Problematic: A Feminist Sociology*. Milton Keynes, Open University.

Smith, R. (1987) 'Equal opportunities in management and training', *Open Learning*, 2(3), 36–9.

Smyth, J. (ed.) (1989) *Critical Perspectives on Educational Leadership*. Lewes, Falmer.

Spelman, E. V. (1988) *Inessential Women: The Problem of Exclusion in Feminist Thought*. London, Women's Press.

Spender, D. (1980) *Man-made Language*. London, Routledge and Kegan Paul.

Spender, D. (1987) 'What is feminism? A personal account', in J. Mitchell and A. Oakley (eds) *What is Feminism?* Oxford, Blackwell.

Stanley, L. (ed.) (1990) *Feminist Praxis: Research, Theory and Epistemology in Feminist Sociology*. London, Routledge.

Stanley, L. and Wise, S. (eds) (1983) *Breaking Out: Feminist Consciousness and Feminist Research*. London, Routledge and Kegan Paul.

Tannenbaum, R. and Schmidt, W. H. (1973) 'How to choose a leadership pattern', *Harvard Business Review*, 36, 95–101.

Taylor, H. (1984) 'Sexism and racism: partners in oppression', *Multicultural Teaching*, 2(2), 4–7.

Tong, R. (1989) *Feminist Thought: A Comprehensive Introduction*. London, Unwin Hyman.

Torrington, D. and Weightman, J. (1989) *The Reality of School Management*. Oxford, Blackwell.

Walby, S. (1990) *Theorising Patriarchy*. Oxford, Blackwell.

Warwickshire County Council (1989) *Women Secondary School Teachers in Warwickshire; A Wasted Resource?* Warwickshire County Council.

Weick, K. (1989) 'Educational organisations as loosely coupled systems', in T. Bush (ed.) *Managing Education: Theory and Practice*. Milton Keynes, Open University Press.

Weiler, K. (1988) *Women Teaching for Change: Gender, Class and Power*. South Hadley, MA, Bergin and Garvey.

Weiner, G. (ed.) (1985) *Just a Bunch of Girls: Feminist Approaches to Schooling*. Milton Keynes, Open University Press.

Westoby, A. (ed.) (1988) *Culture and Power in Educational Organisations*. Milton Keynes, Open University Press.

Wolf, N. (1990) *The Beauty Myth*. London, Chatto.

Index